women
and water

Stories of Adventure,
Self-Discovery, and Connection
in and on the Water

women
and water

From the team behind **SHE EXPLORES**

GALE STRAUB, HAILEY HIRST, AND NOËL RUSSELL

CHRONICLE BOOKS
SAN FRANCISCO

*For you, that cracking open this book might hold
the promise of a seashell to the ear.*

Design by Rachel Harrell.
Typesetting by Frank Brayton.
Typeset in Harriet Text and Poppins.

GoPro is a registered trademark of GoPro, Inc.; Instagram is a
registered trademark of Instagram LLC; Slurpee is a registered
trademark of 7-Eleven, Inc.; *Tetris* is a registered trademark of Tetris
Holding, LLC.

10 9 8 7 6 5 4 3 2 1

Chronicle books and gifts are available at special quantity discounts to
corporations, professional associations, literacy programs, and other
organizations. For details and discount information, please contact
our premiums department at corporatesales@chroniclebooks.com or
at 1-800-759-0190.

Chronicle Books LLC
680 Second Street
San Francisco, California 94107
www.chroniclebooks.com

contents

Authors' Notes

Gale Straub, Hailey Hirst, and Noël Russell

A PATIENT SHAPER

Water is a brilliant sculptor. In the Wobanadenok, or White Mountains of New Hampshire, the land of the Wabanaki and Abenaki peoples and the state I call home, there's a feature called the Basin. This smooth granite bowl is 30 feet (9 metres) wide, 15 feet (4.5 metres) deep, and 25,000 years in the making. Franconia Notch, the valley where it sits, was carved by the harsh and icy movement of a glacier. Over time, a river teamed up with sand and stones to sculpt the Basin. It's a masterpiece, certainly, but it's also a work in progress. Handling a material like granite takes patience, its rough edges polished in tiny increments rather than with the flourish of a scalpel.

Just as it carves our landscape, water shapes us in ways both overt and covert. Everyone has a unique and personal relationship with water, one that ebbs and flows over time. I didn't think much of my own growing up; in many ways I took my easy access to water for granted. I can still recall long, hot summer days spent waiting for my dad to get home from work so he'd take me and my siblings to Loon Pond for a swim. The deep well on our property that provided us with fresh groundwater that Dad would use to spray his vegetable garden and Mom to paint her watercolor lilies. The spring in the woods where we'd fill gallon jugs on Sundays, the waterfall we stumbled across on a forested trail, and the rainbow trout we'd catch standing on the same frozen pond I'd swum in just months earlier. Whether or not I knew it then, water shaped me all the same.

GALE STRAUB

HAILEY

Water is versatile. For all its subtlety, it is equally destructive—a force that has the power to take away all that we hold dear. But it also provides: sustaining and renewing life as we know it. There is so much about water's significance that is difficult to articulate; it's no wonder that we invite it into our lives through activities like surfing, sailing, river rafting, and walks by the ocean. It's as if a closer proximity might help us understand its gift. And yet, up to 60 percent of our bodies *are* water. So maybe we're simply seeking answers to ourselves.

—GALE STRAUB

women and water

CONNECTION & IMPERMANENCE

My memories of growing up in Central Idaho on the lands of the Shoshone-Bannock muddle together like watercolor paints bleeding onto a dry page. If I close my eyes, I can still smell cottonwood trees and hear the constant sound of rushing water somewhere nearby.

I spent my childhood summers traveling between a few watershed valleys. These valleys are all linked by highways that run parallel to the rivers' bends before they cross alfalfa fields kept green by ticking sprinklers. I drew the life cycle of salmon in pink crayon at a school just five miles from the Boise River. I floated the Payette River at summer camp, waded the Salmon searching for caddis fly eggs with my entomologist grandpa, and learned to fish in springs that fed the Snake with worms dug from my grandma's garden.

These rivers, and the snowmelt lakes and creeks that feed them, have imbued my life with a sense of impermanence, and also one of connectedness. As they quench the high desert and link our inland lakes to the Pacific Ocean, they also tether each generation in time with the next, and the next. Oh, that endless flow.

Now that I live in a lakeside city in the Syilx/Okanagan territory of British Columbia, I miss the energy of the rivers, but I'm closer to the snowpack and the seasonal shifts that mark the passage of time here. My first daughter was born in the winter, and I'll never forget our first tender outings on snowshoes with her in tow, imagining warmer days and yearning to follow the rivers back to the lakes of my youth.

—HAILEY HIRST

authors' notes

JUST LIKE WATER

I've spent most of my life living near the coast of Northern California. The shoreline and the icy waters of the Pacific have always been a place for gathering—whether it's nets full of fish or family convening around a beach bonfire. The ocean has always filled me up in ways that nourished and strengthened. When I was young, my mother used to bring me to the shore and tell me to toss my worries into the roaring waves. She said the Ocean was big enough to hold all our troubles in her giant blue belly and that when the swells are calm, She reminds us that no matter how many concerns we carry, we still have the power to be at peace. These days, the sea is like an old friend to me—the place I often go to feel grounded and find healing. I visit her shores and cast my cares into the rolling waves. I've found that some forms of stress are water-soluble.

My adoration of aquatic adventures has had many iterations over the years, from lifeguarding at local pools and waterfronts and working as a swim instructor and coach, to late nights spent swimming laps at my local community pool—escaping the bustling sounds of the city with each dunk of my head. My waypoints through life have been marked by water: wading through the San Lorenzo River while holding my grandma's hand, my very first backpacking trip beside the headwaters of the San Joaquin River, teenage bonfire-filled beach nights, the smell of chlorine in my damp hair while sitting in morning college classes, late-night runs along the Hudson after long days at work as a young executive, and slow summer weekends spent blowing bubbles with my nephews in my sister's backyard pool. Water has been the backdrop to every cherished memory, the soundtrack to unforgettable experiences that shaped me. Swimming will forever be my favorite form of dance—because there's no fuller feeling than moving fluidly through the medium that brings me the most joy.

—NOËL RUSSELL

NOËL RUSSELL

The Source

Time in the outdoors has become more important than ever. Nature offers us space for stress relief and grounding. It provides opportunities to connect more deeply with the world around us, as well as to tap into our inner selves for reflection and growth. Between the impact of a global pandemic, the escalating ripple effects of climate change, and persistent political turmoil, we've come to further understand the soothing balm of nature as both a necessity and a precious resource.

In particular, we've noticed that women are increasingly seeking outdoor activities, exploring close to home, and finding new angles of familiar places. We're looking for different ways to step outside, more space to do so safely, and sensations that help us feel something novel. While water access differs by region, many of our cultures and civilizations are built around it. Yet due to a number of circumstances (many of which we'll touch upon in these pages) we may not have fully embraced the potential of this element for recreation.

Putting a paddle into the lake you normally see from afar, zipping up a wetsuit for the first time, plunging your head under the surface of a chilly ocean . . . all these water-centric acts offer fresh perspective, a different mode of travel, or another dimension of "home" to discover. And as you'll read, this book is about more than just what we do in the water. It's also about the connection and healing it helps us channel, as well as the importance of protecting it for years to come.

We also want to honor water as a source of livelihood, nourishment, and a way of life. Just like the women featured in these pages, it is multifaceted. Truth be told, we could easily create a book that solely focuses on women surfers or paddlers or marine biologists. But we chose to touch on the many connection points women have with water to highlight the possibility it holds, as well as to embrace how it permeates and propels our lives in different ways.

In showcasing women who are in various stages of their water journeys, we hope to inspire you, the reader, to consider all the ways you can dive in and deepen your own relationship with waterways near and far. We also hope these women's stories will empower you to learn more about ways to protect this element we hold dear. Within these pages you'll find first-person stories of women from around the world, as well as practical how-to sidebars interspersed throughout to pique your curiosity and give you some of the tools you need to set out on your own.

The book is organized into five sections that embody the powerful dynamics of water:

- **Testing the Waters:** Just dipping your toe in? You're not alone. Learn from women who are trying new things in and on the ocean, lakes, and rivers. We also invite you to jump in and gain inspiration from those who have devoted their careers to conserving these bodies of water for years to come.

- **Diving Deep:** Discover divers, underwater photographers, and other experts in their fields, as well as personal stories that reveal the depth of the connection we have with water.

- **Channeling Potential:** Develop a deeper understanding of the healing and transformative nature of water and those who are harnessing its potential benefits, be it through entrepreneurial ventures, guiding others, innovations in science, or personal endeavors.

- **Finding the Flow:** Creatives, surfers, river rafters, and ice-skaters all have a drive to seek out and embrace flow in their work and play.

- **Merging at the Confluence:** When more than one river comes together, it meets at a confluence and creates something new. The same can be said for the women featured in this section, whether they are multisport athletes, multidisciplinary professionals, or community builders.

There's no one way to read this book: You could devour it all in one sitting or pick it up from time to time for inspiration. No matter how you approach it, we hope this book, and the women within, serve as a reminder of all that's possible in, on, and around the water. Now let's dive in.

Testing

the Waters

The JOY of SWIMMING

As an Olympian, swim instructor, and water safety advocate, Karin knows the importance of being comfortable and confident in the water. Which is why she founded Water Safety Antigua, an organization dedicated to educating the community on water safety and preventing drowning.

Being in the water feels like the best hug I've ever received. I feel secure and at peace—it's like a comforting embrace. I want everyone to be able to experience that same feeling.

I live on an island—we're surrounded by water—and yet, so many of my fellow Antiguans don't know how to swim. So, I founded Water Safety Antigua in hopes of educating more people on water safety, and showing them the joy of swimming.

Once, I was teaching this woman how to swim and was helping her float on her back. Floating on your back is challenging for many. It's a vulnerable experience—letting go and allowing yourself to trust something new. She was a bit worried, so I took some time assuring her and validating her feelings. Then she took a breath, leaned back, and began to float.

She closed her eyes and the biggest smile formed across her face. I still think about that moment often. That experience is exactly the reason why I do what I do: so more people can know what it feels like to be held by the water.

Swimming has always been a big part of my life—one that means so much to me. It's not only a great way to exercise and a fun activity to do with others, it's also a life skill. Swimming teaches us a lot about ourselves; it builds strength physically and also mentally. I dream of a world where everyone in my community has an opportunity to learn to swim—to challenge themselves to discover a new skill, no matter what season of life they're in. You're never too old or too young to learn anything, and everyone deserves to feel safe and welcome in the water.

—KARIN BROWNE

EXPERIENCING WEIGHTLESSNESS

Lizzy is an Oregon-based public health professional, outdoor enthusiast, and watercolor artist. In 2019, a climbing accident left her paralyzed from the chest down. Since then, she experiences the outdoors differently than she did before.

I cannot begin to tell you the freedom of floating.

Having always identified very much with earth, it's notable how much water has become a major theme in my life more recently. Since my climbing accident in 2019 when I was permanently paralyzed from the chest down, two of my major hobbies now are watercolor painting and swimming. Both, in their own way, bring me weightlessness: one, through transcendence into a space of hyperfocus where it's just myself, my brush, paint, and paper, and the other where it's literally the only time in my life now where I can defy the heaviness of my unresponsive torso and limbs and just float.

I've always been a planner. I always knew exactly where I wanted to be one month, one year, or five years from now. My accident was a massive upheaval to all of this. To put it bluntly, C1 and C2 cervical fractures had me a whisper away from death. Three months in the hospital and many more months dependent on assistance while I figured out independence again forced me to give up control. All of my plans for the future were thrown into the shadow of uncertainty.

Eventually, I started to see the horizon again and, with it, an opportunity to set a new focus and intention in life. An early goal, inspired by another adaptive athlete, was to try two new adaptive sports a year. As a new wheelchair user, you get the benefit (and challenge) of starting nearly every sport from zero no matter how skilled you were at it before. It's a great opportunity to give things a shot you wouldn't have thought yourself capable of or interested in in your "previous life." Swimming, it turns out, is now something I really love. I think we as humans are so predisposed to routines and sticking to our comfort zones. At the risk of sounding very, very cliché, there's so much in this world to experience, and life is too short.

testing the waters

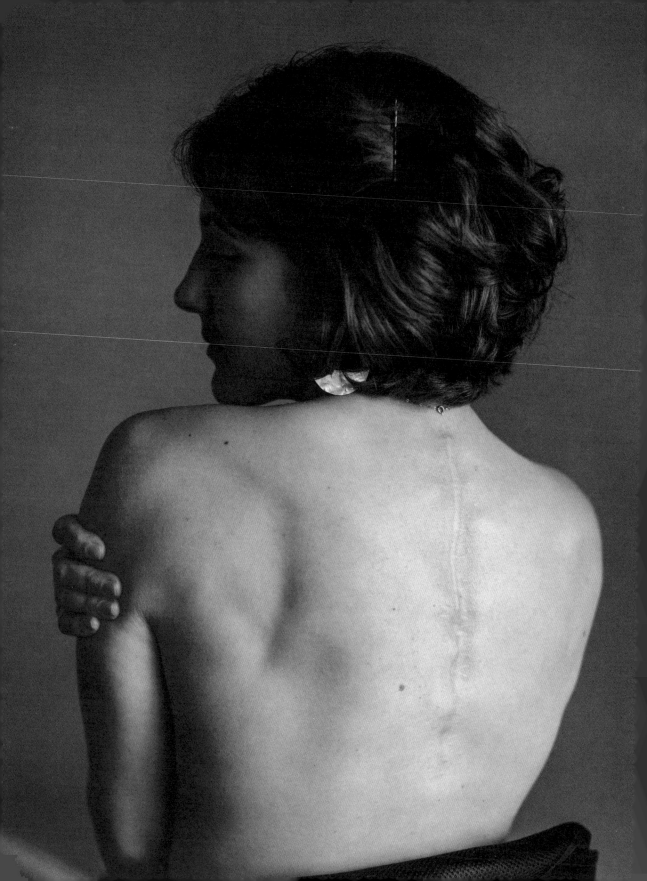

Watercolors are not a comfort zone. To work with watercolor, you have to give in to its uncontrollable nature. In so many ways that I'm still coming to appreciate, working with watercolor is like living life. You control what you can, and you let the rest unfold. You have to find beauty in the chaos. Each time I put my brush down on a blank piece of paper, it's like asking, "Where will we go today?" When you see my art, perhaps you'll see indications of this delicate dance I still do. My struggle for precision and control, and where the paint has reminded me that sometimes the best thing you can do is let it flow.

—LIZZY RAGAN

RESILIENCE *in* DIVERSITY

A marine biologist, educator, and deep-sea ecology enthusiast, Mugdha has worked aboard ocean vessels and on rivers monitoring salmon. She champions community engagement in science and conservation.

The first time I tried snorkeling, I was nineteen years old. I put on my mask, snorkel, and fins near a shallow seagrass bed and slid into the warm water of the Caribbean. I swam around for about an hour, completely in awe of all that I saw: the way the seagrass was "waving" underwater, how the light danced through the water column, the small fish darting about, the lone lobster or sea urchin hiding in the seagrass . . . I was hooked and knew I wanted to spend as much time underwater as I possibly could.

I started my career as a marine biologist studying coastal and deep-sea fish. When I was in graduate school, I realized I was interested in both research and science communication because they complemented each other. I became passionate about helping people connect with marine environments through community-based science, stewardship projects, and educational outreach.

Earth's aquatic ecosystems (both marine and freshwater) are incredibly diverse. When I think about how these environments relate to each other, I immediately think of iconic salmonids in the Pacific Northwest. Many salmon species are anadromous, which means they live in both salt and fresh water depending on their age and life cycle stage. These fish are a wonderful reminder of how fresh and marine habitats are connected! Almost every land mass has interconnected rivers and streams that link us all to the ocean. What we do upstream further impacts what happens downstream.

I enjoy engaging in community work to restore aquatic environments, whether it's through beach cleanups, monitoring water quality, planting native trees, or conducting salmon surveys. We can all make a difference in our local communities and create lasting, meaningful change.

Our work isn't done once habitats recover or improve—we need to continually protect and support biodiversity in nature (in water and on land). We also need to focus on interdisciplinary, collaborative solutions, such as creating robust policies, monitoring ecosystems, getting communities involved in stewardship projects, rallying support for environmental causes, and most important, bringing diverse perspectives to the table—because nature thrives and is more resilient when there is diversity.

—MUGDHA FLORES

EXPERIENCE AQUATIC ENVIRONMENTS LIKE A SCIENTIST

You don't have to be a trained scientist to study organisms, environments, and the interactions between them. In fact, adding simple scientific practices to outdoor pursuits can connect us all more deeply with nature.

How can you practice experiencing environments like a scientist?

OBSERVE: Observation is essential to the scientific process. Rather than merely noticing, observation calls us to analyze in greater detail, either by our own sensory perceptions or with the addition of tools like thermometers, magnifying glasses, or goggles to see underwater. Take this as an opportunity to slow down, get closer, and notice *more*—above, below, and all around you.

ASK QUESTIONS: Next, deepen your observations with inquiry. You don't need to form a hypothesis to ponder the whats, hows, and whys when you're encountering things you may not have examined that closely before. Let your curiosity lead the way.

RECORD YOUR FINDINGS: Log what you observe in a notebook, an app, with your camera, microphone, sketches, and so on.

INTERPRET: Bring your discoveries home and compare them to your own previous notes or others' findings in field guides, history books, blogs, and the like to gain context and interpret what they might mean.

SHARE: The bonus step: share your recorded observations with scientists, organizations, or research projects, and engage with the scientific community! By sharing your findings, you can contribute to real research projects, providing invaluable data to people who are professionally studying certain aspects of environments.

What is community, civic, or crowdsourced science?

Community science is the practice of public participation and collaboration in scientific research to increase scientific knowledge. Usually done via volunteering, people share and contribute to data monitoring and collection programs.

Data collection might include taking water samples; recording temperatures; reporting whale sightings; measuring water levels; tracking marine debris; monitoring algae or cyanobacteria blooms, animal activity, and plant life; reporting invasive species; measuring precipitation and weather patterns . . . the list goes on!

Many international scientific organizations, government agencies, universities, and natural science museums have ongoing opportunities for amateur scientists. To find out how you can help in a specific aquatic environment, look locally first. For a wider scope, the National Oceanic and Atmospheric Administration (NOAA) maintains a citizen science and crowdsourcing database, and organizations like Citizen Science and SciStarter are accessible anywhere online. There are also opportunities via apps like iNaturalist and the Audubon Bird Guide.

Community science increases access to knowledge, provides unexpected insights, advances research on a scale that would be otherwise impossible, and encourages people to take a stake in the world around them. And on a personal level, it is empowering!

The next time you head out to the beach, swimming hole, or local wetlands, consider engaging with community science. You don't know yet what you might spot through a pair of binoculars, or hear with an ear to the ground, or witness in the rocky shallows that, surprisingly, teem with life. Happy observing!

FIRE *and* WATER

Gina is a Latine scientist currently working toward a PhD in forest and fire ecology at University of Washington School of Environmental and Forest Sciences. As a former NASA Geoinformatics Fellow and professional cartographer, Gina uses a suite of remote sensing tools to analyze changing patterns of wildfire, identify climate-resilient forest structures, and understand effects of management on fire severity across western North American forests.

Everything is connected, and we are all part of the landscape. No process acts in a vacuum.

Fire and water are both vital, regenerative processes that can also be enormously destructive given the context and right combination of environmental variables. Both fire and water are essential for life on this planet, yet settler colonial culture has villainized fire in ways that water isn't really subjected to.

So much of the West's current fire situation is a direct result of fire as an ecosystem process being removed from the land. Can you imagine if we removed water from the land? If we somehow decided to ban it? If we looked at floods and hurricanes and raging rivers and decided that water was simply too risky? We've essentially done this to fire: Fire

has been a critical ecosystem process for thousands and thousands of years—forests *need* fire—but colonial forest management practices have removed it from the landscape for long enough that we're starting to deal with very serious consequences.

There are so many connections between fire and water and how they regulate each other. But what really excites me is thinking about how we might build a culture of respect for fire the way we've built a culture of respect for water. What if we saw *both* fire and water as vital to our forests, and to our lives? Fire is a tool, a resource, and a cultural practice. There is no such thing as "bad fire," only fire that has negative effects.

Humans have been, are, and always will be key participants of every ecosystem.

testing the waters

The people indigenous to these lands—the first stewards of the land—know best how to maintain ecosystem resilience. That knowledge is critical if we want to even consider how to go about restoring ecosystem balance and function under rapid climate change. Modern conservation as a practice is only necessary in a culture built around extraction. There is no need to "protect" lands in a culture that doesn't try to destroy them.

—GINA ROSA COVA

LOOKING UPSTREAM

As an environmental scientist and avid outdoor lover, Morgan spends her weekdays monitoring the water quality of the Sacramento—San Joaquin River Delta aboard a research vessel and her weekends hiking far and wide in search of crystalline lakes, rushing rivers, and icy streams in the High Sierra.

I feared the water for most of my early life. The eerie afternoon shadows in our backyard pool, the mysteries beneath the surface of the turbid lakes near my home. Trips to the beach were always spent hugging the shoreline, only dipping my feet, while the rest of my family enthusiastically submerged themselves in the waves. But as I grew older, I recognized that water is an element equally as beautiful as it is dangerous, and this notion has led to a tremendous respect that resides deep within me.

Though my daily work is focused on the delta, I've been grateful to learn so much about the way water moves—starting high up in the Sierra Nevada and traveling west toward the Pacific Ocean. And as a hiker and backpacker, I've found a deep appreciation in happening upon the fresh lakes and rivers that ultimately lead to the brackish waters I'm so familiar with. Experiencing those high alpine environments makes me feel more connected with the work I do downstream and leads to a greater understanding of how everything connects—and what we, as humans, can do to help.

As a resident of California, I can speak to how familiar many of us are with the term *drought*. We're told to limit showers and water our grass less frequently. I consider myself lucky to be able to see, firsthand, how drought affects water quality. Yet, as I watch fresher environments become saltier, and observe the struggle of resident critters as they attempt to adapt, this privilege can often feel like a burden.

I carry that home with me and feel the weight of it with every washed dish and every watered plant. And while these realizations can become taxing, I also believe the constant recognition of our impact on the Earth is what makes a good environmental steward. I think we can all benefit from viewing our relationship with water as one that is built on respect. One where we are more mindful in regard to conservation and more reverent of this precious element that is so vital to our lives.

—MORGAN BATTEY

testing the waters

FUN ON THE WATER WITH FURRY FRIENDS

If your life is enriched by animal companionship, you probably already fold them into most of your routines and interests. But if you're looking to add something new to your life—whether that's a new puppy or a paddleboard—here are some tips for bringing pets to the water:

RESPECT YOUR PET'S PERSONALITY: Some pets will love swimming, while others won't. Some might prefer to relax on a lake's edge instead of wading into its waters. And some are better suited still to staying home. You'll probably be able to gauge how adventuresome your pet's personality might be.

TAKE BREED AND ABILITY INTO CONSIDERATION: Generally, dogs are more willing to get wet than cats, but some breeds like Bengals, bobtails, and Maine coon cats like swimming. As for dogs, short snouts and swimming don't mix, since water can more easily go up noses and pose a drowning risk. Plus, some body shapes are more adept at floating and maneuvering in the water than others.

EASE INTO THE WATER: Hanging around, playing games, or taking a favorite toy to the shoreline and in the shallows before getting in to swim, float, or paddle can aid in encouraging your pet's comfort. Help them get used to new, large gear by letting them sniff, nudge, and step onto them as they wish. When it's time to board a boat, get onto a board, or wade in a bit deeper, take things slowly. Watch for signs of fear or anxiety and honor them.

PERSONAL FLOTATION DEVICES (PFDs) ARE KEY: Collars are dangerous to pull on and harnesses don't offer the support and buoyancy that PFDs do, which come with sturdy handles that make it easy to swoop your pet up in case of going overboard or other incidents.

BE AWARE OF ENVIRONMENTAL RISKS FOR YOUR PET: Not only can light or speckled noses, ears, and bellies get sunburnt easily with added reflection from the water, the dynamics of water environments themselves can pose other risks. Stay aware of currents, sneaker waves, riptides, or rocks, and ask a ranger or lifeguard for specifics. Blue green algae blooms, or cyanobacteria, are another hazard—for you and your pet! Look up reports prior to visiting, and when in doubt, stick to colder, moving water.

FOLLOW ALL POSTED GUIDELINES: Bring pets only to beaches or recreation areas where animals are allowed, obey leash laws where required, and always be mindful of neighbors. If going off-leash, make sure to brush up on recall skills to ensure your pup will return to you whenever needed!

CONSIDER THE IMPACT OF YOUR PET'S PRESENCE: Our favorite waterways are home to many creatures who also deserve to find safety and comfort there. Carefully observe where you plan to set up for the day so you can keep a respectful distance from local wildlife. Don't move driftwood or logs and keep barking at a minimum. It's also important to follow Leave No Trace principles and pack out what you pack in, including poop.

BELONGING *in* *the* WATER

Sophia is a pre-med student who enjoys adrenaline-rich adventures through which she has developed a newfound passion for water sports. Most recently, she has immersed herself in diving and surfing—both activities that allow her to feel an incomparable sense of peace and freedom.

When I was in elementary school, my parents surprised my brother and me when they informed us that we'd be getting a pool in our backyard. This was not only a big deal for us, but also for my parents. As immigrants from Haiti, this act was their way of giving us a piece of the American dream. I remember my dad showing me how to breaststroke in the water and me doing handstands every chance I got. Joy and satisfaction filled my body during those experiences in the pool.

However, I didn't feel completely comfortable in the water until more recently. For some time, I felt a sense of anxiousness before I entered an open body of water. I worried about my ability to tread and

relax. In addition, I didn't want to embarrass myself in front of strangers or my friends. These feelings challenged me to learn more about swimming—to work on moving past my fears and becoming more resilient. Spending more time in the water has also exposed me to the lack of racial diversity in water sports and activities.

Growing up, I didn't see my reflection in others when spending time in the water. There is a significant disparity in the Black community regarding water safety and education, often stemming from systematic racism and stereotypes. I felt limited in my swimming abilities and knew I wanted to explore that arena more. I also

knew it was important for other Black and Brown people to see a familiar face doing things they might be interested in doing. I hope to aid others in becoming more comfortable in the water, just as I received help on my journey.

Today I am working on getting my scuba diving certification, and I hope to get into free diving. Surfing is also something I would like to improve on. The joy I feel while participating in these water sports inspires me to continue pushing my own boundaries as the years go on. For me, exploring and going on adventures has been and will always be a reminder of things bigger than myself. I aim to encourage people around my age and older, but more importantly younger generations, to feel comfortable and confident enough to try whatever they can imagine. I hope they realize that regardless of their skin color, they too belong in the outdoor world.

—SOPHIA EUGENE

Diving

Deep

CAPTURING *the* DIVINE FEMININE UNDERWATER

Jamie is a self-taught photographer offering fine-art underwater photoshoots in Los Angeles under the name "Birdee."

I started doing self-portraits during a difficult time in my life. I felt very discon-nected from myself and my intuition. Having a creative outlet to focus on felt very cathartic, and to my surprise, the self-portraits grew to become an incred-ible tool for helping me feel more con-nected with my body, my emotions, my creativity, and my voice. I was mostly taking self-portraits in the privacy of my home, discovering my emotions and my body in a new light with each click of the shutter. I had a pool at the time, and one day as I was swimming I had an epiph-any that I wanted to incorporate my love for water in my photos and highlight the light, ethereal, and feminine element that water provides.

Many things converged to draw me to water, from growing up in Florida and having nightmares ever since I was a child about tidal waves and being sub-merged, to allowing myself and my voice to emerge through my underwater art. As a photographer, I see things through my lens of history, experiences, and desires, and I believe all these factors play a role in my passion for this work. I have found a way to rewrite my nightmares into beauti-ful imagery while also empowering others to feel embodied, beautiful, connected, and brave.

Because I believe all bodies are beautiful and worthy of being art, I do what I can to create a safe space for my subjects to

explore liberation and the divine feminine. By *liberation*, I mean letting go of rules and constructs, allowing the body to feel free and move in new ways. By *divine feminine*, I mean an appreciation of the feminine energy, which is not at all connected to gender. We so often go through our lives on a schedule, focused on achieving. The feminine energy is connected to the body. It's nurturing, soft, heart-centered, sensual, and related to cycles of creation and transformation. I hope that anyone experiencing a shoot with me or simply seeing my art can feel closer to these energies.

There is always a feeling of playfulness during my underwater shoots. For some women, it's been years since they allowed themselves to be free and play in the water, diving and doing flips. The water has a way of holding them, making them feel safe and not so exposed.

—BIRDEE (JAMIE JOHNSON)

diving deep

GET STARTED WITH UNDERWATER PHOTOGRAPHY

Taking a camera underwater is bringing a portal to another world. It's a way to capture light and color, suspend movement, and document breathlessness. It's both an artistic medium and a tool to communicate what's discovered down below.

While professional cameras and housings can be a big investment, and the techniques can take time and training to learn, dabbling in underwater photography is also possible for the casual photographer or curious swimmer. Here's how you might take to your local pool, spring, or stone-bottomed lake with a camera in tow.

Pick your starter camera.

WATERPROOF DISPOSABLE CAMERAS: This kind of one-time-use camera typically has a roll of film inside for twenty-seven photos and works up to a depth of 32 feet (10 metres). They also often have a flash, which can help illuminate your subjects if the water isn't crystal clear or the sun isn't directly overhead. These are the most budget-friendly (albeit not earth-friendly, as they are single-use) option, and they're best for low-quality close-up shooting for fun and experimentation.

WATERPROOF MOBILE PHONE CASES: Use the camera you already have embedded in your mobile phone by adding a waterproof housing. It's best to look for one specifically designed for underwater photography, since it'll have more water-tight seals and lens covers than mobile cases made purely for protection against the elements. This option is pricier than the disposable camera, but you'll get a lot more photos without having to buy a whole new camera.

ACTION CAMERAS: You might be familiar with GoPros, but there are a lot of other action cameras out there that perform similarly. Most come with underwater housing and provide the most technical options and highest resolution of the three starter options listed.

Consider water clarity, color, and light.

Not every body of water or overcast day is ideal for underwater photography—especially when you're starting out with more basic equipment. Light and visibility are important, so here are some things to understand and plan around:

CLARITY OF THE WATER: Any silt or suspended particles, or even bubbles from flow and falls, will affect what your camera can capture. The cloudier the water, the closer you'll need to be to any subject.

WATER CASTS A COLOR: Blue, green, and yellow tints are common underwater, and even if your eyes see the vibrant colors of a fish or underwater fauna, your lens may not quite capture it. Red filters are one way to help overcome this.

LIGHT AND WEATHER CONDITIONS: Clear skies and a high sun will illuminate deeper into the water and provide you with the brightest lighting conditions for basic cameras. And the deeper you go, the darker it gets!

Choose your subject.

What are you drawn to capturing? Does your location have interesting submerged objects, creatures, or features? Are you wanting to capture a body in motion or specific sport? Think about how to get up-close or interesting angles of whatever you're interested in. If you're hoping to photograph wildlife, this is an opportunity to learn more about the ecosystem you're exploring and how to respectfully interact with all the life within it.

Dive in and photograph.

GUARDIAN *of the* SPRINGS

Michelle is a professional mermaid and free diver born and raised in Mexico. She now lives in Florida, where she's involved in the local mermaid community and activism to protect Florida's freshwater springs.

To me, being a professional mermaid means being a servant and champion of the water. The word itself has *maid* in it, and I do feel a duty in performing as this magical creature. In most of my shows, I promote water conservation and educate people on how to take care of this natural resource.

When I became a mermaid, I initially just wanted to learn how to take pretty pictures underwater. I looked up to other mermaids and what they were creating, so I began doing research on how to take underwater photos and learned about the discipline of free diving, or diving without breathing equipment. Eventually I got my free diving certification. Now I use the breath-holding techniques I learned to tap into the mindful and meditative aspects of diving, and make engaging videos that capture the wonder of the magical springs.

Florida has the largest concentration of freshwater springs in the world. These flowing springs are home to unique species, migratory fish, and manatees in the winter months, as well as significant archaeological finds. Without this water, Florida and the bountiful life it sustains would cease to exist. Unfortunately, these vital springs are in grave danger. They face pollution, the overpumping of the aquifers that replenish them, development, and sea level change. Many are gone or destroyed already.

Like many Floridians, I lived here for many years unaware that these majestic wonders of the world existed. When a friend introduced them to me, I was immediately hooked. Since then, I've been inspired to swim in them whenever possible and research ways to get involved in protecting them. I now volunteer with the Florida Springs Council and Florida Springs

Institute, have participated in documentary projects, and use my platform as a mermaid to raise awareness for the dangers they face.

These springs are sacred and magical. The water is a constant 72°F (22°C), which might feel chilly to most people, but I find it refreshing. When I submerge in this water, which is some of the purest and clearest water on earth, I feel transported to another dimension where nothing else matters but my presence in the water, and I surface feeling cleansed, healed, and rejuvenated.

—MICHELLE COLSON

INTO *the* DEEP

Kasie is the director of Applied Water Science at the Monterey Bay Aquarium, an internationally known nonprofit public aquarium dedicated to inspiring conservation of the ocean. In her role, she's tasked with working on the chemistry, microbiology, instrumentation, life support engineering, and environmental science for water discharge. She loves diving, sailing, and spending time simply being in the water and soaking up all the feelings that come with it.

There's a magical aspect to water that can't be studied—it just has to be felt.

I grew up in Georgia, nowhere near the ocean, but with parents who always encouraged me to be outside in nature. When I was a toddler—and not yet able to swim—we were camping in the mountains and visited a fish hatchery. When my dad turned his back, I jumped into one of the trout ponds and he had to pull me out. When questioned about why I would do such a thing, I told him matter-of-factly: I just wanted to be with the fish.

As the Director of Applied Water Science at the Monterey Bay Aquarium, I have a front-row seat to the reality of how critical water is to countless ecosystems, organisms, and our livelihoods. And as fun and fascinating as it is, it's a responsibility I take seriously. There are so many lives that depend on the water we're providing and taking care of. It's also water that comes right out of Monterey Bay, as our facility is literally connected to the ocean. I can see what's going on in the bay by looking at our own water systems. Harmful algal bloom? Yep, it's in our filters now. Sewage spill up the coast? Better check the microbiology in our tide pool. Having such a close connection with the water outside our walls, while we take care of the critters within them, also makes me hyperaware of mundane things that can have big impacts—such as where car wash water goes; the impact of leaving the tap running longer than I need; why we shouldn't use copper rain gutters; and the impact the brine from home filtration systems has on our ground water.

diving deep

One of the most fascinating parts of the job is being able to create healthy environments for animals that no one has ever seen before. The *Into the Deep* experience at the aquarium has been one of the most rewarding challenges of my career. So many brilliant people worked to create a novel and complex life support system that mimics the water in the deep ocean. For us water scientists, this meant developing a system capable of very low oxygen levels, low pH levels, and frigid temperatures. We spent years studying the water chemistry in the deep sea and learning how to create it inside our walls.

The success we've seen in being able to keep animals healthy and on exhibit that have never been seen before by the public is extraordinary. Tears came to my eyes when the first beautiful jellyfish went into one of these exhibits and began to thrive. The deep sea is a beautiful, wonderful, alien world—one that I never thought I'd be able to work so closely with. And now we get to share it with millions of other people who hopefully will feel that same sense of wonder and desire to protect these precious environments.

—KASIE REGNIER

FINDING FREEDOM *in* SWIMMING

Bonnie swims all over the world and has written extensively on water, climate, and the natural world, including two books on those topics: *Why We Swim* and *Sarah and the Big Wave*. On any given morning, you're very likely to find her swimming or surfing near her home in Berkeley, California.

I'm usually in the ocean at first light to surf. It's my quiet time to think and notice things: the stars winking and giving way to day, the cold fingers of water reaching into my wetsuit, the way the colors change as the sun inches closer to the horizon. Once I start hunting for waves, it's all I'm thinking about. I'm attuned to the swell as it approaches, where the peaks are, where I have to paddle to get into position to take off on a wave. It's very absorbing. It's lovely for keeping me acutely in the present.

From my research for writing *Why We Swim*, I also know that the feeling I have in water stretches back in time, connecting me to what it means to be human. We emerged from the water at some point in our evolutionary past, but we haven't relinquished our desire to be near it. We can't swim from birth, but we tell ourselves stories and myths about the water and how we might learn to conduct ourselves in it. Stories are how we pass down knowledge—the hazards around water, the skills of swimming—but also meaning.

Growing up, my swim team was very diverse—it drew kids from different racial and socioeconomic groups all around Long Island. It expanded my view of what community could look and feel like. Up until the time I joined the club, I had a bifurcated experience of life: the predominantly white world at school and in the town where I lived, and the Chinese immigrant community that was my extended family network in Flushing, Queens, and Manhattan's Chinatown. Every week for Sunday dinner, we went to visit my grandparents' house in Flushing, and it was filled with aunts and uncles and cousins and friends, all of

whom were Cantonese. I often felt caught between worlds. But on our swim team, we weren't "the Chinese kids"—we were a family of champion breaststrokers. We had the freedom to forge our own identities in the water.

Today, when I think about my own two growing sons, I wish for them to have a healthy respect for and understanding of the dangers that might be present in the water so that they can always find ease and joy there. I want them to feel free.

—BONNIE TSUI

diving deep

BECOMING *a* MERMAID

Irene is a free dive instructor, mermaid instructor trainer, cofounder of Plus Size Scuba Girls, and the only woman PADI (Professional Association of Diving Instructors) Course Director in Quebec. She is passionate about supporting self-expression and building supportive and inclusive communities through aquatics.

Water is my life. I can tell when I'm away from water too long because my mental health takes a serious nosedive. Swimming is the perfect way to completely disconnect from your "real" life. There is no gravity weighing your shoulders down. I feel free—no pain, no stress, nothing. Just me and the absolute peace that comes with the special kind of silence you can find only underwater. Everything just stops.

I can't remember not being obsessed with water. Growing up I spent every day, all day, in the pool. I fell in love with mermaids from a 1975 anime movie called *The Little Mermaid*; I just wanted to be the main character. I used to play "mermaid" in the local pool and discovered synchronized swimming after watching one of the best teams in the country practicing for a show for the Monaco monarchy. I thought to myself, *Wow, dancing in water and being a princess?! Count me in!*

I truly enjoy incorporating the creativity of synchronized swimming and the flow state of free diving into my mermaiding. Whether I don a full tail, makeup, and accessories, or just slip on my monofin, I immediately become a mermaid. And when you're a mermaid, it doesn't matter your size, your gender, whether you're neurotypical, or what your orientations are. That's what I love most about being a mermaid: It's for everyone. It can be like playing dress-up, it can be a highly athletic activity, and it can be cosplay. It can also be a way of discovering or even reinventing yourself. And even though so many people might find it absolutely and completely ridiculous, once you try it, I promise you can't help but enjoy it.

—IRENE MARCOUX

LETTING LOCALS GUIDE *the* STORY

Inka is a UK-based wildlife filmmaker, underwater photographer, and technical scuba diver, with a background in marine biology. She's traveled the world with her work, collaborating with scientists and locals in conservation and storytelling.

Filming wildlife in the water creates a host of challenges. I can't sit in a hide and film on a long lens the way you can on land. Divers have to navigate currents, work with a limited supply of air, jump between gas mixes, and plan for complex decompression stops.

The most important thing for me when filming is that the diving itself feels second nature. When I am completely at ease 30 metres (98 feet) or more below the surface, I have the opportunity to focus on the most incredible underwater displays: like when a shark turns and looks you straight in the eye, or a manta ray races across the reef only to hang above you.

The filmmaking process can start months before I'm actually in the water. Studying my target species—its behavior, its role in the ecosystem, and its current threats—all play a huge role in the way I approach a shoot, the style of imagery I hope to achieve, and the narrative I aim to build.

The way I frame a shot in the water may be because I want the species to feel small in a vast ocean or I may want to emphasize a unique adaptation or ability. But no matter how much I plan my shots or the story, I always need to be ready to adapt and capture the unexpected.

In my journey as a filmmaker and ocean conservationist, I have learned to allow the communities and wildlife I work with to guide the story. Ocean conservation is a complex issue; every coastline is unique and so are the communities that line their shores and the issues they face.

While I love being able to travel to faraway places and experience a variety of marine interactions around the globe, some of my most memorable encounters have been in my home waters off the United Kingdom. Swimming among the kelp forests off the coast of England feels like being in another world. Our kelp forests support a huge variety of life including the gray seal, one of my favorite species to interact with. Often people have no idea that an entire forest and an incredible blue shark population is waiting just off the coastline, and are even fearful of the idea that there are sharks in our waters. Yet understanding our local waters is vital, as we are in the best position to act as their guardians.

—INKA CRESSWELL

diving deep

LEARNING *to* BREATHE

Zandile is a free dive instructor, swimmer, scuba diver, and the founder of the Black Mermaid Foundation in Cape Town, South Africa. Her work and storytelling is expansive—deepening how local ocean-facing communities relate to water and conservation.

Diving in the kelp forest is like traveling through the unknown worlds of all the fantasy books you've ever read. I duck dive into these golden forests that darken and morph, where a shark might be hiding in the shadows. Each time I'm there, I feel in awe of the sheen of the leaves and the way the light and shapes of this moving waterscape can fully change from day to day.

Teaching others to dive is the ability to show someone a portal to paradise and let them explore this incredible place for themselves. All I can do is hold space for their fears, assuring them that I am with them, and that they can lean into this discomfort to experience magic. I find diving deeply spiritual, and so it is an honor for me to take this journey with anyone into the water.

Ever since my first snorkel trip gave me the opportunity to see beneath the surface of the water, I've been seeking more of that feeling of belonging and expanding into

what it meant and what it could be. Learning how to free dive has been a journey of healing and becoming. First, I learned how to breathe. Then, that the diving line in front of me was all that mattered: the here and now. Finally, I learned that in order to dive—and in order to be true to myself—I would have to be vulnerable, and for the first time, it was safe to be.

Growing up as a Black woman, I was taught to be strong enough to endure it all, and in part, to tolerate violence as a means to succeed. I grew up with high walls inside violent systems that stripped the humanity of my Blackness.

The ocean was the one place where I didn't have to be strong, where for all my ambitions, she required me to pause in order to be with her. The underwater quiet brought me to the internal work of unpacking all the stories of fear—about water, about achievement, about success, about myself. She made me realize that uncertainty was a good place to be, and

diving deep

that darkness was a good place too . . . that you could revisit all your fears and not run from them, but see them and acknowledge their presence as part of the journey. And somewhere in all of this was the release of everything the world had told me I needed to be. I could just be me, and here, and that was good enough.

To be largely underrepresented in the ocean/outdoors space is hard. Breaking norms and tendencies that cater to one kind of "explorer" comes with challenges. In showing up, in advocating, and in experiencing the general hard that life can be, I sometimes don't know how much more I have in me—but the ocean pours energy into my body to try again.

And so, whether I am holding my breath at the bottom of the ocean, or breathing through a harder moment on land, I have learned that discomfort is a good thing. These moments that threaten to kill us transform us into a newer version of our being, strengthened by love.

—ZANDILE NDHLOVU

Channeling

Potential

NO ME *without* WATER

Carin is a disabled writer, ice swimmer, and professional boudoir photographer. She lives and swims in the waters of Western Massachusetts, where she constantly scouts secret brook baths and secluded stream pools to soak in.

My relationship with water feels too entire for worded descriptions. I could say that I feel a joy seldom afforded to disabled people dealing with chronic pain by playing in summer's rushing rivers. I could say that I experience profound healing from interacting with the icy waters of dead winter. I could say that to feel weightless and at the whim of currents, tides, and temperatures year-round is uniquely freeing and empowering, and that it has awakened a fuller sense of some deep-rooted feminine knowledge in me.

Water is utterly mesmerizing in its ability to glint, trickle, tickle, crash, seep, erode, puddle, flow, freeze, steam, spray, splash, push, and pull. The visual aspect alone is beautiful enough some days to keep me in those freezing temps for longer, not minding the numbness creeping into my toes in exchange for a unique view of ice forming in front of my eyes from the spray of a waterfall.

There is no sense that is not engaged to its fullest, no cell that is exempt from the feeling of immersion, no thought that is left unsoaked from a dive below the surface. With every swim, I am returned, connected again to the earth and the simultaneous ancientness and newness of water, every cell in my body tapped into its powerful, natural truth. In giving myself to this revitalizing practice regularly, I have evolved and connected myself more deeply to the ecosystem around me.

In the water, there is some silent switch in my brain that gets flicked. It's a moment of freedom—freedom from my chronic pain and the ongoing trauma it causes. This freedom is small, mere minutes in a day, but it is everything to me. It's obvious to me that to be in wild water is to be home, the fullest and deepest sense of home I've ever found. There is no me without water.

—CARIN TERESA

COLD-WATER SWIMMING SAFETY

Any cold-water swimmer can attest to the euphoria that follows an icy dip in open water. Whether it's increased mental clarity, decreased pain, or an elevated mood, the benefits of cold-water swimming can be felt immediately; many swimmers testify to the amazing way they feel. This is partly due to the endorphin rush triggered by plunging into uncomfortably cold water but can also be attributed to the thrill of adventure. Whatever the benefit, cold-water swimming is worth trying, but it's important to be well prepared when doing so. Here are some helpful tips to safely experience the thrill of the chill:

GO TOGETHER: The buddy system is essential to safe swimming. Not only does sharing the adventure help keep one another safe, it also makes it more fun. Brave the plunge together or take turns monitoring each other's swims from the shore. When swimming together, keep close to each other, stay observant, and swiftly take action if you see your swim buddy struggling.

PLAN YOUR SWIM: Research the spot where you intend to swim. Get familiar with hazards such as currents, boat traffic, wildlife, and obstacles such as rocks or fallen logs. Check the water's temperature if you're able to, and keep a close eye on the forecast. If there's a possibility of inclement weather, reschedule your swim for another day. Before venturing out, let someone know the exact coordinates of where you're headed and what time you intend to finish—better yet, bring a third person along for the ride.

KNOW YOUR ABILITY: Assess your swimming skills and be sure you have the ability to complete your intended swim. Once in the water, continue to check in with yourself, and go with your gut if something doesn't feel right. Always swim close to shore in order to ensure the ability to exit quickly if conditions change or you experience muscle cramps. Sticking close to shore also helps avoid dangerous aquatic traffic and allows your swim to be easily observed by others.

COME PREPARED: Practice helping a swim partner out of the water and assisting them in getting warm. Pack ample blankets and towels and keep an emergency communication device nearby (in a bag or in your parked car) along with a form of identification. Know the signs of hypothermia and take a CPR course, if possible, to bolster your safety skills. Bring along necessary gear, like a swim cap and goggles, but also consider investing in a swim tow float as an extra safety aid.

START SLOWLY: Never dive or jump into cold water. Instead, take a minute to let your body adjust to the temperatures. Entering the water slowly helps give your mind and body time to adapt. Start with short swim sessions and always keep your time in the water brief. If your body still feels cold after several minutes of swimming, exit the water and get yourself warm.

KEEP MOVING: Upon exiting the water, dry your body immediately, bundle up, and keep your muscles moving—jump in place or go for a short jog on the shore. Keeping your body dry and active post-swim helps reduce risks and makes your wind-down time more comfortable. Never take a hot shower after your swim; rather, make sure you have plenty of cozy clothes, and pack a thermos of a hot beverage to aid in keeping your core warm.

FISHING *for* CONNECTION

A fly-fisher from Maple Valley, Washington, Penny has had a long career as a public involvement practitioner consulting on infrastructure and civic planning decision-making that often considers water quality, abundance, and conservation. Penny grew up swimming in New Hampshire, but it wasn't until her brother invited her to fly-fish in her thirties that she started recreating in water again.

They say trout don't live in ugly places, and that is indeed the case. On a day in May, I left Seattle, hauling a 27-foot (8-metre) travel trailer behind my SUV, with the intent to be gone for five months and to fly-fish my way across the country. I did that and lots more.

My journey, which a friend named "Penny's Pescatorial Pursuits," took me through twenty-nine states. I fished in sixteen of them. I wandered a lot. If something was of interest, I would go to it, regardless of how far "out of my way" it took me. That's why, perhaps, my cross-country trip was 18,000 miles (29,000 kilometres) long! I fished a good many of the rivers listed in every book about "places you should fish in the United States before you die."

As a member of a terrific online women fly-fishing community, United Women on the Fly, I posted when I might be in an area and sought fellow women fly-fishers who might want to meet up and fish together.

I made connections with numerous women—fishing with fellow women anglers in Oregon, New Mexico, Idaho, Utah, Montana, Wyoming, Wisconsin, New York, and Vermont. Without fail, every woman was welcoming, helpful, competent, and joyful. I can never fully describe how wonderful it was to find and spend time with so many kindred spirits. Of all those women I fished with, I had met only one of them in person before the trip. The generosity, kindness, and support I found were incredible.

And the waters—oh, the waters I found. The crystal clear, cold tailwaters of the San Juan River in New Mexico where you could see every fish within a stone's throw of the boat. The sun peeking over the rim of the canyon walls, illuminating reflections on the mirror-like water of the Green River in Utah. The snow-covered, sparkling mountains that keep watch over the Bitterroot River in Montana. The lakes that are surrounded by amazing, other-worldly rock formations in the Black Hills of South Dakota. The endless, lush green of the Driftless in Wisconsin. The beauty was overwhelming.

But my journey wasn't all roses. I'm an extrovert on steroids, and spending days on end by myself, as I explored astounding natural places (Yosemite, for one), awe-inspiring cultural and historical sites (Chaco Culture National Historical Park), and impressive architecture (Chicago), left me feeling lonely. I found myself happiest when I was on the water, fishing with a new acquaintance. People ask me if I would do another similar journey again. My answer is always the same: "Yes, but not by myself." Even the water, as much as I love it, doesn't replace that human contact for me.

I was married to the love of my life for thirty years. The last eight years of our marriage, my wife suffered from chronic and progressive liver disease. I worked full-time to support us and was her caretaker when I wasn't working. Occasionally, as I was able, I would slip away for a few hours of fly-fishing to refresh myself so I could step back into the day-to-day challenges her illness brought us.

Eventually, the disease took Barb before she could get a new liver. I was devastated by her death. Needing space, my brother and I took my trailer to Idaho and spent a week camping and fishing on the St. Joe River. Being in the water, totally present, gave my grief room to breathe.

Being in that river, surrounded by unimaginable beauty, helped me rediscover the good in life. Watching beavers swim along, eagles fly overhead, and deer saunter by helped me understand that life is a procession. Sometimes you proceed on your own, sometimes you're lucky enough to walk with someone you love, but regardless, life will unfold as it should and our best purpose in life is to live fully. That is what the water does for me. It makes me feel part of the great procession of life.

—PENNY MABIE

A SEA *of* ABUNDANCE

As a food columnist living just steps from the ocean on the central coast of Oregon, Katie enjoys encouraging her readers, as well as her own family, on how to respectfully forage and harvest seasonally available food, and have fun doing it.

I've always been surrounded by water.

When I was a teenager—dealing with typical teenage stuff—I would regularly drive to Dahl Beach in Gladstone, Oregon, to sit along the edge of the Clackamas River and gather my thoughts. There was something about that moving water that I endlessly craved because it so easily quieted my mind and calmed my soul.

These days I am constantly around water—from the Pacific Ocean to the Alsea Bay, to the Alsea River, to the small creek that flows through my yard. Sometimes I'm chasing albacore tuna 50 miles (80 kilometres) out on the ocean, jigging for bottom fish along the dangerous rock piles, or reeling in a fighting chinook salmon. Other days I'm catching crawfish along the river with my little ones, watching them splash and play, soaking up the sun. For me, being surrounded by water means being surrounded by abundance of all kinds: peace, energy, and life.

I believe that when you have a direct connection with your food, you develop a greater understanding of the unique ecosystem it takes to grow it, what sustainable consumption means, and what effect consuming those foods has on your body. All these are of vital importance to the health of ourselves and our planet.

By developing recipes that have been inspired by my time spent around water, I hope to encourage people to have a true connection with what they eat and a deepened appreciation for nature—for getting outside with friends and family, breathing fresh air, feeling rays of sunshine on your skin, and experiencing the simple joys of sharing a meal together.

Strengthening the bonds of love, finding tranquility in the outdoors, and being recharged with an urge to do it all over again—that's the power of water.

—KATIE WILEY

IMMERSED *in* SWIMMING

Eden is an open- and cold-water swimmer based in London who works with numerous international swim and adventure brands to advocate for LGBTQIA+ Rights and Visibility using her Instagram platform, @TheTransgenderSwimmer. Wild swimming has taken Eden to some of the most beautiful waters in the United Kingdom.

I often joke through winter that I'd be more than happy not to swim and just turn up for the post-swim coffee and cake. In truth, I adore the feeling of being immersed in the water regardless of the temperature, and to date I've never not swum when given the opportunity to do so. Swimming is the activity I use to socialize and keep fit. I'm able to check in with myself and process difficult feelings. It's helped me connect with thousands of other swimmers and adventurers who share the love of water.

Swimming the equivalent of a marathon in the Jubilee River 10K was something my ego pushed me to do. A lot of the training was routine but also exciting, as I was constantly swimming farther than I had before. I remember one morning it was very difficult to train; as soon as I got in I felt cold and like I wouldn't be able to complete my 6-kilometre (3.7-mile) planned training swim. I was kind to myself and stopped after a few hundred metres. During the actual race, I became very tired at 8.5 kilometres (5.3 miles) and felt like I wouldn't be able to complete the distance. I pushed through, knowing that finishing before I had given absolutely everything would be something I would regret. With the support of friends and family, I made it to the finish. I was amazed a week later when I found out I was the first openly transgender woman to compete in and complete a swimming marathon!

LGBTQIA+ rights differ from country to country and even sport to sport. At a recreational level, those from the community can struggle to find access and to feel comfortable when taking part. Knowing this, and having experienced discomfort at times myself, pushed me to use my voice to do more. I love hearing about people's first swim experiences, especially from those who didn't think that the water was for them.

One message that lives with me was from a woman called Emily who was recently out as trans and just getting into outdoor swimming. Just the weekend prior, she'd worn a swimming costume out at a fairly quiet beach for the first time and loved the feeling. After two weeks of talking, Emily shared, "You showed me that I could just go swimming and enjoy myself and the world wouldn't explode! I thought I was 'supposed' to wait years before being comfortable with swimming, as that seems to be the standard trans thing, when in reality I did feel comfortable; I just thought I was supposed to pass first." Emily now swims both outdoors and indoors. She has become her own advocate for inclusive access and also advises her employer on how to do better.

I would like to continue seeing sustainable change within our community. Brands are now starting to recognize the responsibility they have to not only support but advocate for equality for all in the water. Many people within the LGBTQIA+ community have intersecting identities and heritage, and it is important that all these are recognized so we can all enjoy the water if we wish to.

—EDEN ELGETI

channeling potential

COLORS *of* COASTAL CULTURE

Michaela is a watercolor artist and Indigenous kid lit illustrator. She was awarded a 2021 Caldecott Medal for her work on *We Are Water Protectors* by Carole Lindstrom, and continues to paint and mentor other illustrators in Alaska.

Creating art is an act of reciprocity, a way to express my gratitude for Mother Earth. It becomes a reaction, a conversation, one way in which I can help defend her.

I first began illustrating picture books a few years ago with one of our local tribal organizations. They were creating books by Native people for Native people, and it was an opportunity I embraced. I've always been drawn to storytelling in its various forms, and as Lingít people, we come from a rich and powerful storytelling tradition.

Picture books spoke my language like nothing before had. They became a way to reconnect with my culture, find my artistic voice, and give back to the Native community in a unique way. I feel very grateful to be doing this work. I'm one artist among many who are working today to create respectful and accurate representations of Indigenous peoples.

Children's books are reflections of our society. They communicate who is visible and important in today's world. Therefore, representation that reflects the very diverse experiences of Indigenous peoples is much needed. In this country alone, there are nearly six hundred federally recognized tribes as well as many others, each with its own unique stories. It is deeply inspiring and engaging work, and I want to keep working to honor and uplift Native people from all nations.

I am of mixed Lingít and northern European heritage. I identify most with my Lingít heritage, as I was raised on the traditional territories of my ancestors surrounded by family and culture. That being said, I have many privileges as a white Native person and continue to learn and unlearn in order to better serve our communities.

The coastal wilds of southeast Alaska, traditional territory of the Lingít, Haida, and

Tsimshian nations, inspire me on a deep level. We are nestled in the Tongass rain forest—a labyrinth of islands and waterways, mountain ranges, and ice fields. Life is oriented around the relationship between land and sea—a theme I seem to be constantly drawn to.

I work to capture the feel of this environment, whether it's through the seemingly endless shades of blues, greens, and grays, the way mist and light interact with the trees and waves, or the beautiful animals and plant life that call this region home. My mind is usually lost in the magic and ethereal beauty of this place, and I'm always on the lookout for moments that move me and the stories they inspire.

Visual storytelling can stir up powerful nostalgia for family and place, a theme I believe to be integral to who we are as humans. I love the personal connection it can create between so many strangers. We all love stories!

—MICHAELA GOADE

The OCEAN *as* UNDERSTANDING

Sofia is a Korean-British athlete, presenter, and science enthusiast who finds rest and healing swimming and scuba diving in salt water.

Like water, the mind can only reflect when it is still.

I get stressed and overwhelmed easily. I think that's part of the reason why I find the natural world so compelling—it's just so much bigger than I am, it takes me out of my own head. In water, I can just be. The phone can't ring, I don't have to talk to anyone, the earth-bound world can't reach me. My racing thoughts disappear. Ocean is all there is, all the way to the horizon, and nothing outside of that exists.

I was fascinated by the ocean from an early age. I loved the way it looked and moved. I loved the way it made me feel about myself when I was in it: untethered, present. I was always curious about science and the natural world, and was lucky to follow that curiosity beneath the surface when I started my scuba diving journey at age thirteen. Up until that point my relationship with water had been entirely playful. Learning to dive introduced a healthy amount of fear into that relationship. Water is powerful and unpredictable, and I had to respect what I was playing with. Still, the ocean inspired my creativity in the best way. Every time I slipped beneath the surface I felt as if I were escaping into another world, and those experiences made their way into my writing: tales of epic fantasy and faraway lands. As I grew older, that sense of sanctuary became increasingly important for my mental health.

In 2021, I was diagnosed with complex post-traumatic stress disorder (C-PTSD). With this comes periods of deep depression, interpersonal struggles, and an intense loneliness.

When we're struggling, we want to feel understood. It's no use for people to tell you to stay positive or that it'll get better. You don't see it in the moment; in the moment you just want someone who gets it, because that means you're not alone.

I've always wanted to feel understood more than anything. For me, the ocean is that understanding. In her, I see myself.

She is as ever-changing, as light and dark, as wide and wandering as I am. I think the ocean understands what it means to be human. Even if I'm alone with her, I never feel lonely.

When things get bad for me mentally, I take a train out of the city where I live and go drift in the sea. It's cold, but I feel like I'm with someone who understands, and who, for the moment I'm with them, can bring me right back *here* without ever saying a word.

My relationship with water is, in one word, *homecoming*. It seems ironic because one might think I'm escaping home by seek-ing out the sea. But no word more simply describes the feeling that water takes me back to my roots, as a human and as Sofia.

—SOFIA JIN

FINDING HEALING
in NATURE

Judith is a therapist and the owner of her own trauma-informed practice, Triune Health & Wellness. She bathes and swims in rivers and lakes as part of her mindfulness practice. Judith calls the land of Confederated Tribes of Warm Springs, also known as Central Oregon, home.

When I talk about the ways water has been healing for me in my personal life, it is important to understand that it is not a story that exists outside the context of history.

Predating colonial times, West Africans were considered the world's best swimmers. West Africans grew up around the ocean and their lives revolved around bodies of water. The connection to water in West African cultures was not only recreational, but also symbolic as a healing and spiritual element. In fact, the use of water continues to be an important element across the African diaspora, as well as in many other cultures around the world.

Throughout the European and American history of chattel slavery, swimming and water activities started to shift among African Americans. Swimming went from a recreational activity and practice that was embedded in African roots to becoming a survival skill for those who were used

as property during the era of enslavement. Enslavers began to look at Black Americans' ability to swim as a threat to their created structure in society. As a result, swimming was discouraged and prohibited by enslavers to keep enslaved peoples from running away.

Since then, there have been many policies and intimidation tactics that have impacted Black people's access to swimming. Some included segregation laws of pools and beaches, as well as violent intimidation tactics toward Blacks who entered segregated pools. White flight, when white people began leaving increasingly crowded cities for suburban neighborhoods, gave rise to an increase in private pool club areas and home pools being built. The public pools that remained began to shut down, making it even more difficult for Black people to access pools.

My relationship with water today involves intentional practices that are connected

channeling potential

to my ancestry. Yes, I have enjoyed certain water sports like paddleboarding, kayaking, Jet Skiing, tubing, and some other fun activities. I will say that the consistent activities that have been healing for me involve intentional mindfulness practices that connect to my roots. Activities like bathing nude or clothed in a river, praying and meditating in water for ceremonial purposes, creating an altar that honors my ancestors using water as an element, and creating baths with different healing herbs, essential oils, and salts, have supported my mental and physical health in more ways than other activities. They empower me in my identity by acknowledging the trauma that my ancestors experienced throughout history and by recentering some of the original healing practices of my ancestors before the colonial era.

This way of being with water and intentionally incorporating it into my life today increases the confidence I hold in my identity as a descendant of West Africa and as a woman. These mindfulness practices allow me to feel grounded and centered even in the midst of chaos and confusion. They have also allowed me to experience spiritual healing that comes from my African roots rather than from a Westernized American lens. It empowers me to heal generational trauma and reconnect my body to the powerful healing elements in water regardless of what activities or practices I am doing.

—JUDITH SADORA

channeling potential

FLUIDITY *in* RECOVERY

Antoinette is a Black, multicultural water sports enthusiast who calls northern Colorado home. Among many titles, Antoinette is the executive producer of WhitewaterTV, cofounder of Diversify Whitewater, and a paddling team member with both Team River Runner and Badfish SUP. She's also the architect of the free National American Adventure Sports Club.

After seeing a poster for the national organization Team River Runner on the wall at my physical therapist's office, I came to water sports. At the time, I had a caregiver, a service dog named Phoebe, and a walker helping me with everyday tasks. Unfortunately, a broken back, traumatic brain injury (TBI), and degenerative arthritis that began in my thirties left me unable to care for myself. I'm fifty-four now, but when I was twenty-three years old and serving in the U.S. Army, I broke my back and injured my head and shoulder in a rappelling accident in South Korea. After eleven years of military service, I was an army veteran. I was looking for something to bring me back to life and good health. So I showed up with my walker and service dog, and within a few short months, I was part of the whitewater paddling community.

A TBI, much like post-traumatic stress disorder (PTSD), is a condition that most in the medical community believe you can never fully recover from. Unfortunately, I also think this is true. But sports such as kayaking and stand-up paddleboarding on moving water require focus, quick information processing, problem-solving, decision-making, confidence, courage, and planning. It's a social sport too. You have to develop friends and create connections because you cannot or should not boat alone. All these skills have helped heal my brain and body while making me a more social person.

It is not easy being a disabled athlete. My disability is hidden and people sometimes don't have patience when I forget things or require slower verbal instructions. Also, when I don't paddle for a while, I forget everything that I've learned about kayaking.

Recently, I had to take almost two years off from paddle sports for surgery and

recovery. When I finally returned to kayaking, I didn't remember the names of my gear, the sport's jargon, or how to hold my paddle. I had to start over from the beginning and learn everything as if I were a new paddler. I had panic attacks sitting in my kayak in my garage, and I wondered if I'd return to paddle sports. During the darkest moments where the negative self-talk kicked into high gear, I remembered the No Barriers USA mantra: "What's within you is stronger than what's in your way." I repeated this to myself, out loud, until I began believing it again. The power of neuroplasticity and positive self-talk is incredible.

But honestly, it was a commitment to safety boating at the UrbanTrekkers summer camp for a group of Black, Indigenous, and People of Color (BIPOC) youth that ended my panic attacks on the water. Being committed to showing up for those little ones to demonstrate that we in the BIPOC community are outdoorsy made me brave. That day on the water with youth BIPOC paddlers helped me tap into my warrior energy.

Since becoming an all-around sportswoman, I've reversed the outdoor recreation narrative. Today, this Black, multicultural woman routinely takes white people on backcountry and wild and scenic river trips and teaches ice fishing. Hopefully, one day, when other rafts pass by my expedition, they'll see me and not assume that one of my white friends dragged me into the outdoors. Instead, they'll ask, "So, which one of you won the river lottery and brought your river buddies out on the Main Salmon River for a five-day trip?" I take so much pleasure in helping everyone enjoy the health and social benefits of water.

—ANTOINETTE LEE TOSCANO

INCLUSIVITY *in* AQUACULTURE

Imani is an oyster farmer and scientist passionate about improving the health of shellfish populations in the Chesapeake Bay and abroad. Currently, Imani is enrolled at University of Maryland's Center for Environmental Science, Horn Point Laboratory. She is also the founder of Minorities in Aquaculture, a nonprofit committed to championing women and diversity in the aquaculture sector.

My family has lived on the eastern shore of Maryland for centuries—from Rock Hall, to Chestertown, to the lower parts of Cambridge and Crisfield—and since the 1800s everyone's primary work has been in commercial fisheries. For generations, both sides of my family have worked as watermen.

And yet, I always wondered why I had never seen another woman or man of color in leadership roles in aquaculture. I remember learning about a Black-owned oyster farm from a Netflix series called *Chef's Table*. That was the first time I ever saw a Black oyster farmer in my six years of working in the industry, and I finally felt I wasn't alone. That moment changed my life and was the catalyst that spurred me to create Minorities in

Aquaculture (MIA). I wanted to give others that same feeling of being seen by bringing together a powerful network of women of color who want to further their impact on the aquaculture industry.

Recently, MIA joined the cohort of minority-owned organizations that wanted to stand up for diversity, inclusion, and active minority engagement. Seeing other minorities step up in their own fields of marine science assured me that I was on the right track. My vision for MIA is to empower and support women of color of all ages in their careers in aquaculture. I want to encourage them to push past the barriers that people of color face while promoting access to valuable resources to

channeling potential

help them achieve their dreams. Whether it's through creating paid internships or helping people acquire the gear, housing, or transportation they need, MIA is building a well-rounded support system aimed at upholding the longevity of these women's careers in aquaculture.

When I'm on the water, it's like experiencing the most comforting *hello* I've ever felt. And that feeling motivates me to do more: to share that experience with women of color who haven't yet felt seen or accepted in that way, or those who have and deserve to feel it so much more.

—IMANI BLACK

Finding

the Flow

On WILD ICE

Laura is a professional wild ice-skater, skating instructor, and multidisciplinary creator. She's based in Colorado and has skated on high mountain lakes across the globe, including the Himalayas, where she works with locals in Nepal to introduce ice-skating to the mountain communities.

Every day on wild ice is unique and fleeting. Sometimes you can see the bottom of the lake around the shoreline or schools of fish swimming beneath your blades as if you're in a glass-bottom boat. The water changes color with depth. You might also find artistic ice formations like intricate frozen bubble forests, aquatic plants, or oddities dropped in the lake over the years—and what's discovered one day could be covered in snow the next.

Skating is a passion that helped shape my identity. I began skating at six years old, then teaching at fifteen. I competed for Penn State and tested through the highest levels with U.S. Figure Skating. But when the demands of my graphic design career took over after college, I didn't know where skating fit in my life anymore. I didn't have time to maintain my skill set, and I fell out of love (and touch) with the sport.

Instead, I became enamored with hiking in the mountains on the weekends while living in Colorado, quickly taking to hiking fourteeners (14,000-foot [4,267-metre]

peaks). One winter while on a snowshoe hike in the Indian Peaks, I saw pristine mountain ice in a gorgeous alpine environment and wished I had my skates. Ever since then, I've been hiking with my skates, seeking out new wild ice each winter. Through these experiences, I rediscovered my love, excitement, and inspiration for figure skating.

After an injury kept me from practicing jumps for a few months, I went back to the roots of figure skating. Nowadays, the sport is so focused on jump and spin evolution that most people don't know the term *figure skating* is derived from skaters creating "figures" and patterns with their blades on outdoor clear (black) ice.

I got wrapped up in trying to figure out "special figures," which are designs from the 1700s and 1800s. They're extremely hard, so it was a new challenge to perfect these intricate shapes. I also began making design adaptations that worked better with the way our skate boots have evolved and I started designing my own.

The figures I skate are wiped clean when the ice reglazes overnight, but I try to photograph, video, or sketch what I've created in my notebook. In those mediums the art lives on, even if it doesn't remain on the ice itself. Practicing the same movements over and over again locks in muscle memory for me. The repetition of the tracings on the ice are ingrained, and I can recall them in my mind and feel them in my body when I look at the designs I've documented. I'm not sad they disappear. It's amazing to come back to a fresh canvas the next day.

Capturing these moments in photography and film is a way I make my "figures" last longer—and take others skating with me. I didn't expect my videos to go viral on social media, but they've reached hundreds of millions of viewers globally. As my platform has grown, in many ways I feel I've been called to educate and inform. A lot of people are fearful of ice, but I think the more you embrace your curiosity with it, the more it gives back to you.

The ice feels like home to me. I feel safe because I've come to have a deeper understanding of it: knowing why some ice is stronger and weaker, when in the season it first freezes, and when it's no longer reliable. I notice how heat and cold spell patterns melt, break up, and refreeze the ice again. I'm also trying to understand, in the greater scheme of things, how climate change specifically affects freezing of certain lakes and rivers—like the bodies of water where skating originated which no longer freeze—so these exhilarating moments can be enjoyed by generations to come.

—LAURA KOTTLOWSKI

NAVIGATING WHITEWATER

Ash is a river guide who has rafted close to 9,000 river miles since they started guiding in 2015. Ash calls the Appalachians of Northeast Georgia home but has commercially guided in Utah, Colorado, the Carolinas, West Virginia, and beyond.

My body is the tool I use to navigate the river. My body has taken a beating from every angle when it comes to whitewater. My body has recovered in ways I didn't think it could. My body lifts, climbs, grips, paddles, breathes, swims, and empowers everything that is needed to be out there.

I absolutely love whitewater. The first time I went rafting, I knew it was going to ruin any hope of a regular picket-fence life that my parents might have had for me. It keeps me challenged, moving, and on my toes. Each day is different, even if I'm on the same river every single day. The challenges are not only in the whitewater itself, but also in getting people safely down the river and showing them the best time. There's nothing like watching someone else fall in love with whitewater.

In my earlier years of guiding, I took Pete, one of my very special friends, rafting.

After all the larger rapids of the day, we came upon this long and flat section of water, so we jumped out of the raft and floated side by side. Pete said something that has stuck with me for many years. "Life is a lot like the river, ya know? Sometimes there are wild and crazy and unpredictable rapids to get through. Sometimes it's just a nice, calm ride—like right now."

What a simple and obvious statement. But it's a part of my feelings toward life in general. Sometimes we're in a situation that seems like it cannot be navigated. Class V, big waves, dangerous rocks. But even if the boat flips and we swim, we're going to figure it out. We have to.

In many ways, I feel that my existence in the whitewater industry, and in the outdoor industry more generally, is fulfilling my goal of normalizing all body types in the outdoors. I ignore the negativity and

finding the flow

discrimination I've received in person and online. It honestly doesn't matter because it doesn't affect my relationship with the outdoors.

It took me a long time to realize how much I love this body of mine. No matter what anyone else says or thinks, it doesn't matter. The only opinion of my body that matters is mine. They aren't the ones paddling these boats and taking entire waves with their chests. Why wouldn't I love it? Why wouldn't I be proud of it? What other people deem bad, I deem a blessing. My size is an advantage in many ways. I see myself in my own light, not through others' uncaring eyes.

—ASH MANNING

HOW TO READ A RIVER

by Heather Hansman

Heather Hansman is a former raft guide, freelance journalist, and the author of *Downriver: Into the Future of Water in the West.*

If you're paddling whitewater in any craft, from a stand-up paddleboard to a raft, you'll need to learn to read the river to understand rapids and how to move your boat through them. You'll want to know what you're looking at, how rivers move, and how to be flexible once you're in the current.

TAKE A MINUTE AND LOOK: Step one: Pay attention. Take some time to observe the river. Look for obstruction. Notice where it pools and where it flows fast; those signs will help you navigate.

KNOW YOUR HYDROLOGY: All river features are formed by an obstruction in the channel—most often a rock. The feature it makes depends on the flow. That means that rivers can change significantly depending on the water level. For example, a rock without much water flowing over it is just that, a rock. When you have water in the current, and it flows over that rock, it forms a hole, or a hydraulic, when the water recirculates. You generally don't want to hit those, because they can stall or flip your boat. When you have even more water, it can rush over the rock without getting stuck, forming a wave.

LOOK FOR SIGNS: So how do you know what's a hole and what's a wave? The river will tell you, and this is where reading water gets interesting. A hole, rock, or obstruction in the river will grab the water, forming what's called an upstream V. There will be a notice-able point to the feature, with whitewater running away from the point. You'll want to avoid those or be tactical about how to hit them. Instead look for downstream Vs, the smooth tongues of deep water that will smoothly pull you through. An easy way to remember: From above, when you're dropping into a rapid, upstream Vs look like frowns, and downstream Vs look like smiling faces.

WHERE IS THE WATER GOING? You'll typically want to be in the deepest, fastest channel of the river, where the most water is flowing, so look to see where the majority of the river is pushing toward. If you're not sure, try to find some natural signs. Ducks will often naturally find the downstream V in the deepest part of the river. On the sides of rivers, you'll often find quiet backwater pools, or eddies, which are good places to stop.

PICK A LINE: There are two main ways to decide how to run a rapid: You can *scout* or get out above the rapid to look at it, assess the hazards, and pick a line. This is often a good plan on a new river, or when you know there's a big rapid below. Or you can *read and run*, where you pick your line on the fly. This is good for smaller rapids, especially when you're first learning, because you can get a feel for how your boat moves.

ALWAYS LOOK DOWNSTREAM: Whitewater is inherently dynamic, and even the best-laid plans can easily be thrown off when you're constantly moving. Pay attention to the whole river, not just the rapid in front of you, and keep your eyes downriver to see what's coming.

MANATEES, ALLIGATORS, *and* EVERY SHADE *of* BLUE

Yolande spent her early years at the beach, pool, or at the local spring. Today, she spends time paddleboarding on the water's surface and free diving below. She calls Tampa, Florida, home and helps keep the waterways clean by collecting marine debris and garbage when she's out exploring.

I've traveled far and wide, but my home state of Florida holds a special place in my heart. Between the numerous waterways and abundance of wildlife, what's not to love? Florida is seriously captivating. We have spring waters any shade of blue you can think of, enchanting bioluminescent algae, and some of the friendliest gentle giants known to man (the West Indian manatee).

I've been paddling these waterways since 2003 when I was first introduced to kayaking at a marine biology camp. Right away I was hooked; I absolutely loved paddling in my kayak. Fast-forward to a few years ago, stand-up paddleboarding was slowly growing in popularity, and, honestly, I just thought it looked cool, so I pulled the trigger and got my first paddleboard. You

have a way better vantage point while standing, making it so much easier to spot wildlife!

I have alligator stories for days. I really don't know how I still have all my fingers and toes. A friend and I were paddling down one of the only rivers in central Florida that has rapids and just as we hit them she flipped off her paddleboard. At the end of the rapids was a gator hanging on the bank. (Awful timing to be in the water, if you ask me.) I was trying to gather her things and not disturb the gator while she waited in the middle of the rapids. I managed to get her board, shoes, and bag, but before I could get back to her, the gator began drifting toward me. I had to switch boards to keep some space between us. Luckily he lost interest

and made his way down the river and
I was able to get back to my friend. We
saved everything but her GoPro that day.

One of the beautiful things about paddling is that you can access places you
wouldn't otherwise. My friends and I had
always heard about this spring-fed sink-
hole deep in the woods and would drool
over all the amazing photos captured
there. One day we finally mustered up the
strength to do some swamp tromping to
see this gem for ourselves. Boy, when they
say nothing good comes easy, they aren't
playing! Waist-deep in the mud, clear-
ing cobwebs from our faces, and getting
destroyed by Florida's state bird (the
mosquito—go ahead, fact-check me).
Talk about eventful. Once we reached
the edge of the swamp, seeing the bright
blue-green waters gleaming back at us
made it all worth it.

—YOLANDE WEBSTER

A STUDENT
of the SEA

Currently residing on Ramaytush Ohlone unceded land, Olivia is a Mexican American who works as an environmental educator, volunteers with Brown Girl Surf, and serves as an advisory board member for the Explore the Coast Program at the California State Coastal Conservancy.

I feel so fulfilled and complete being so connected with water. I love being a student of the ocean and continuing to learn how water moves, changes, and connects. Without a doubt, the ocean and my consistent relationship with her has deepened relationships I have with other people and the more-than-human world.

The first time I surfed in Mexico was one of my most powerful experiences of joy. I was in the lineup with a few other Mexicanas, and they were so sweet to me. We all shared waves at a perfect left that were peeling along the reef. The water was so warm and I saw a huge black-and-white spotted eagle ray swim alongside me that just took my breath away.

During the fall, at my home break in Ocean Beach, we get perfect offshore winds and incredible sunsets, and I almost always see bottlenose dolphins in the lineup. Each time they come up, I shout with joy and smile from ear to ear, then I catch the next wave.

It can feel overwhelming to acknowledge how climate change is impacting our coastlines. But then I remember the power of our collective imagination, and I envision a beautiful, healthy ecosystem where kelp is thriving, animals are alive, and biodiversity is ever present. I dream about all types of people enjoying the ocean together, with gratitude, a spirit of sharing, and compassion. I also dream about the surf industry moving toward more Earth-friendly materials and away from petroleum, Styrofoam, and other oil-based products. Where surfboards and wetsuits can be biodegradable or recycled: a less

pollutive and single-use industry. I dream about women continuing to make equal prize money for competitions, people with disabilities continuing to have access to the sport, and children of all identities enjoying many days at the beach and their local waterways.

I love the ocean and reflect often on how she has impacted my life so profoundly. I want that for as many people that can also show reciprocal respect for her power and beauty and all the life she supports.

—OLIVIA VANDAMME

finding the flow

MELTWATER *and* WATERCOLOR

Currently based in Berlin, Germany, Larissa is a watercolor artist who works as a researcher in glaciology. She also volunteers as a science educator for the European Geoscience Union (EGU) Cryosphere Sciences Division.

Just before starting my masters in climate change at University College London, I had my first glacier experience on the Langjökull glacier in Iceland. I remember being amazed at how loud a melting glacier is—the cracking, the meltwater running, the wind. You feel as if you're with a living being. It really grounded me and affirmed my desire to study the icy giants of the earth.

Being part of an avalanche rescue mission while working as a ski and snowboard instructor is what first inspired me to also gear my climate science studies toward snow and ice, with a bachelor thesis on avalanches. From there, I moved into glaciological research, and I'm now involved with water resource prediction. Most people don't know that 22 percent of the global population are dependent on snowmelt and glacier melt for their water needs. Even when the research is disheartening and full of problems, I know it's important to predict how melting glaciers will affect water supply, and even if my contribution is tiny, it's something.

I've mainly done fieldwork in the Alps, but it was incredible to be allowed to do it in the Arctic again recently on Nordaustlandet, Svalbard—a part of the world that hardly anyone gets to visit. To see polar bears in their natural habitat, and hear (again: loud!) giant blocks of ice calving off the glacier into the sea is an incredible privilege. It makes you feel alive but also so very tiny, as you're transported into a landscape that is as wild as it has always been.

I'm an introvert, and I need my alone time to recharge, which is difficult to do on a crowded ship in the Arctic. Sitting in a corner of the dining room, painting, was what allowed me to do that during my fieldwork in Svalbard. When I paint, I am in my own little world, an almost meditative state, allowing me to process the day. I'd choose to paint a scene of the day, matching mood and weather, and collectively the daily paintings are a little visual diary of our fieldwork. I gave most of these small paintings away to the crew and fellow researchers as a reminder of this trip.

A quick travel painting captures a feeling, an atmosphere, rather than the details. On top of being portable, watercolor is also suited to the cold and rugged places I favor: it's flowy, it's quick, it does its own thing. Just like the ocean, a glacier, and an avalanche: You're not in control, the water is. You can just learn how to work with it.

Art moves differently than science. It's art that I believe can move people emotionally, make them realize that climate change is not an abstract problem of the future or of other countries, but something that will affect them and their children.

—LARISSA VAN DER LAAN

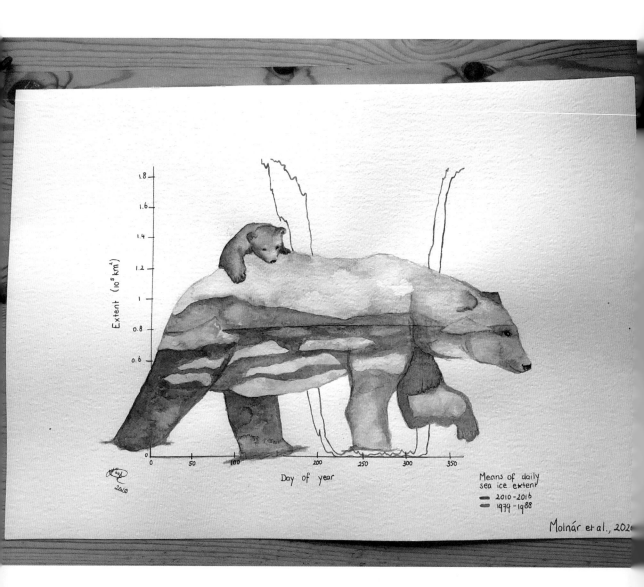

SURFING
through
SEASONS

Rachel is a yoga teacher and surfer in Nova Scotia, Canada, who works with North Preston Surf, a program designed to increase diversity in surfing and to support people of African descent of all ages in Nova Scotia. She is also a mother who surfed throughout her pregnancy.

Surfing as a regular habit and practice changed me. You start to move with the tides and wind changes, learning to honor your own natural rhythms, experiences, and inner knowing. There was a time, in what feels like recent memory, where my fears of the ocean limited the experiences I was open to, or willing to try.

Traveling in my twenties, particularly to El Salvador and Hawai'i, I experienced the surf community and culture for the first time. My initial attempts at surfing were laughable but I couldn't get enough. It felt like years until I saw someone who looked like me surfing, and it was never around my home in Eastern Canada, but I was determined to keep showing up, to exist in this space almost in spite of the naysayers.

My relationship to water shows ancestral and individual healing. Over time, I've experienced subtle inner shifts that transformed into a new ability and awareness in the water.

Most often when I surfed while pregnant, there was no self-imposed pressure to really surf. It was more often about simply being in a wetsuit in the ocean, and continuing to show up as a woman of color. I know at a baseline that my presence shifts the norm, not just as a person of color, but as a pregnant woman in a space still lacking diverse representation.

Surfing after my daughter was born is a beast that I'm still wrestling. Getting my strength and confidence back is a long and challenging process, let alone finding the time and energy to get out there at all. In the beginning, those surf sessions between feedings and naps were life-changing. I was trying to merge these ideas of who I was before motherhood and who I am still becoming. Postpartum surfing provided a needed opportunity to reconnect with myself, even if just for forty-five minutes. The ocean offered a clean slate and renewed energy, my friends were there cheering me on, and little by little I found myself whole again.

Surfing has also brought so many incredible people into my life, as well as relationships that have deeply nourished and surprised me through changing seasons. I don't know who or where I would be without my surf community in Atlantic Canada, who like to frolic in the ocean in the winter, or online communities like Textured Waves, who are creating conscious change for future generations.

When I heard about North Preston Surf, I knew I needed to be a part of this groundbreaking program even though I was living a few hours away at the time. I drove to the surf meetups because I didn't know of any other women of color surfing out here on the East Coast, but I knew how crucial it was for children to see someone who looks like them represented.

Reclamation of Black Joy in the outdoors and especially in the ocean tells a new and vibrant story about our belonging in nature. A lot of days I cried happy tears after the sessions, especially the summer I helped out while pregnant. The whole thing feels so much bigger than me.

—RACHEL BARRETT

FLOATING UPWARD

Among many things, Nikki is a climber, photographer, speaker, educator, and activist. From her home base in Salt Lake City, Utah, Nikki spends the cold-weather months seeking out ice to climb.

Ice is a living, breathing medium. Unlike rock, which really changes only on a geologic scale, ice can change throughout the day, shrinking or growing. It can be as strong as steel or can shatter like glass. It can be dense and "plastic," or it can be like a firm Slurpee. While climbing, you have to be able to read the ice and know what to expect and react to. You also have to learn about everything else around you. Winter weather can change rapidly. Snow can make approaches and descents more strenuous, as well as creating the potential for avalanche danger.

I usually start looking for ice in mid-September in the high country around 11,000 feet (3,350 metres), but it greatly varies as the West continues to warm. I've been ice climbing for twenty-three years in Utah, and wrote the guidebook for the ice climbing here, so I have a pretty good idea of where to look. Once I think there might be a chance of ice, I'll drive up to the Uinta range or Mount Timpanogos and use a long lens on my camera to take a look at a few climbs that I use as a benchmark. If ice isn't present, then I start

looking for other climbs. Overall, it can be a pretty uneventful process: lots of time watching the weather, looking at a computer screen, driving, and hiking. I'm often confused as to why I love ice climbing so much, but it's just a part of me.

Some days are magical: cold enough for ice but still warm enough that you don't need heavy jackets. Days like this can lead to "plastic" or "hero" ice, which your axe and points dig into easily since it's dense and solid. In those conditions, climbing can feel like floating upward. But you can have the opposite experience on the very same day if the weather changes—wind blowing, the snow piling up. Spindrift constantly comes down the route and gets into all your clothing, freezing your face and body. Your hands are constantly above your head and gripping your axes.

When it's really cold, sometimes you can get what we unaffectionately call the "screaming barfies." That's when you get to the top of the climb and finally lower your arms and let go of your tools and the blood returns to your hands. The warm

blood moving through your cold hands causes intense pain that makes you want to put your head in between your legs and just rock back and forth crying. You feel like you are going to throw up and wet yourself at the same time. It's a short-lived experience but one we ice climbers try to avoid.

The variability in conditions is a huge part of what draws me to ice climbing. It's constantly changing, and it forces you to learn and push yourself. I feel very connected when ice climbing. On rock, I can disappear into the movement, but on ice you have to be present. There is so much going on.

When I look back at the last twenty years and counting, a lot of trips stand out. For me, even if the climbing is unique or interesting, what I really remember is who I was with and where. My meaningful climbs were with friends who have since

passed: friends who have been there for me while we were climbing and after-ward, partners whom I trust enough to cry in front of.

I remember being 1,000 feet (305 metres) above a frozen lake when the sun hit the ice and the lake started to "sing" to us as it warmed. Hiking out, the forest white and green, and the sky purple and pink. The mountains in front of us lit up with a rosy alpenglow as we all just stopped to watch. Spotting a cougar running across a snowy slope on the mountain high above us when it noticed us below and stopped and watched us before slinking away. Topping out on the summit ridge of a new climb and hiking to the top because we didn't want the day to end.

Climbing is great, but more than anything it's a means to connect with the outdoors, friends, and myself.

—NIKKI SMITH

INTERTIDAL LIFE *in* MACRO

Jamie is a coastal photographer and tide pool ambassador who leads small, immersive tours of the intertidal zones around the Cape Perpetua Marine Reserve on Alsea and Siletz land near their home of Yachats, Oregon.

The pools have always been the one place on earth where I feel comfortable and a deep sense of belonging. It's an always-changing yet always-familiar place I can escape to and be held, the way some folks may feel about going to a church or temple. Witnessing the symbiosis of all the intertidal life also really helps my heart when the human world feels like far too much.

I've dabbled in photography since I was a young kid who was gifted an old film Minolta camera, but it took a solid twenty years for me to begin to take photography seriously. After years and years of working in aquatic animal husbandry and stifling my creative side, I'm now working hard to make photography my career. I officially started back in 2017 with just a Pentax K50 DSLR and a whole lot of passion and love for the tide pools I grew up around.

More often than not, I'm the person lying heart-to-rocks next to the tide pools, with my feet in the air behind me. My goal is to get as low and close as possible without disturbing the marine locals. I've formed some DIY tools and techniques over the years to help me get vivid, lifelike photos, so I've also been seen with a large sheet of cardboard, kneepads, and more, which always starts some good conversations.

On a personal level, the macro world of tide pools brings me a sense of peace. To witness and learn from so many various species living in a very tumultuous and constantly shifting environment together—that's powerful. In our ever-changing world and climate, I feel a need and almost a responsibility to document these stunning creatures while they are still thriving.

When someone says "I can smell this photo" or "I feel like I'm there," I feel so validated. As someone who left the Oregon Coast for years, I always had a sense of longing for it whenever I wasn't

immediately on the shore. While my photography is very personal to me, I strive to also make it personal for others, to act as an escape or a safe place should they need one.

The tide pool tours are a stellar way to introduce folks up close and personal to the mind-blowing world of these liminal habitats and their inhabitants. It's a whole lot of laughing and joy while we mindfully explore the rocky intertidal zone. To hear the crackling of the barnacles in the early morning minus tides, to feel the rocky protective textures of an ochre sea star, that's the good stuff that creates lasting passion and interest.

—JAMIE KISH

CREATING VISUAL ART TO BETTER UNDERSTAND OUR CLIMATE

by Claire Giordano

Claire Giordano is an environmental artist, writer, and educator who strives to creatively explore the interwoven patterns of people, place, and climate change through her work.

Art—especially painting and sketching outside—is a powerful tool to learn about, observe, and record what is happening to our warming world. While sketching can seem like a simple practice, it requires intense focus on a place and facilitates deep observations of what is happening around us. And this keen observational practice can help us feel connected to the natural environment around us and be curious about how the colors and patterns we paint reflect the impacts of climate change.

SHOLES GLACIER - MT. BAKER
AUGUST 4, 2021

EVERY PATTERN IN THIS LANDSCAPE
TELLS A STORY, AND TOGETHER FORM A PICTURE OF A
RAPIDLY WARMING AND CHANGING WORLD. THE EXPOSED
STRIATIONS OF A GLACIER DETATCHED FROM THE
SHOLES ARE VISIBLE RECORDS OF GEOLOGIC TIME AND
SNOW LEVELS EACH YEAR. THE AURAL PRESENCE OF THE
GLACIER IS MOST STRIKING WHEN DESCENDING THE
TONGUE OF ICE THAT RECEDED   METERS THIS YEAR.
THE SOUND AND SIGHT OF MELTING WATER DROWNS OUT
ALL ELSE IN A CHORUS OF WATER RUNNING ACROSS,
DOWN, AND UNDER THE ICE. IT IS OVERWHELMING
AT TIMES, TO KNOW WHAT THESE AUDITORY PATTERNS
MEAN FOR THE FUTURE OF THIS GLACIER.

THIN & UNDERCUT ICE AT THE TERMINUS,
LIKELY TO MELT BY END OF THE
SUMMER.

THIS PATCH OF ROCK WAS COVERED
BY 38% MORE ICE LAST YEAR. A STARK
BAROMETER OF CHANGE.

EVEN THE YELLOW
MONKEY FLOWERS BY
THE SHOLES OUTLET
INDICATE CHANGE.
AS THE GLACIER
RECEEDS, NEW
PLANTS SLOWLY
FILL IN THE
BARREN GROUND.

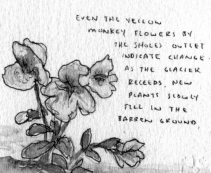

The creative observations of artists of all levels are critical to our collective understanding of the climate crisis and its impacts on our home environments. Next time you hike to a glacier, visit a pond, or explore your local waterway, consider bringing art supplies with you!

Here are some tips for using creative practices to observe and notice environmental change:

MATERIALS: Always bring pencil, pen, and paper. If you have time to paint, add a paintbrush, a reusable paper towel, a small jar for water, and a palette of paints.

GETTING STARTED: First and foremost, don't worry about creating "good" art! You do not need to make a perfect replica of what you see. Not only is this too time-consuming, but it also loses what makes art so interesting: your unique perspective and experience.

THUMBNAIL SKETCHES: Create small sketches to convey the biggest shapes, patterns, and shadows you see in a scene. They allow you to initially explore a place and capture a lot of information quickly (such as the patterns of rocks visible in a newly exposed section of glacial ice).These sketches can also help you plan larger paintings.

LOOK FOR PATTERNS: Climate change is impacting our environment in many ways, and it's worth doing basic research on the regional impacts before drawing or painting a new landscape (such as glacial recession or shoreline erosion). This knowledge helps you focus your paintings on the patterns that illustrate that change.

BE CURIOUS: Whether or not you have the chance to research a place before you arrive, approach the landscape with a spirit of exploration and curiosity. Sketch what interests you and record questions alongside your sketches so you can learn more when you're back home.

ADD WRITTEN NOTES: Record questions, the details of what your five senses perceive, descriptions of the landscape, and observations of your internal emotional experience while you create.

RETURN TO THE SAME LOCATION: Many scientists return year after year to the same research areas to track environmental changes over time. As artists, our paintings and sketches can show these changes too, using a visual language.

A RITUAL *to* RESET

Anna is an artist and author who lives on the South Puget Sound/Salish Sea in Washington. She's an advocate for creativity in all the shapes it takes and champions it on her platform, "Creative Fuel."

I never set out to have cold water be a part of my creative practice, but somewhere along the way, it became essential. Creativity isn't just about making art, but about being curious and open to the world, taking in ideas and letting them marinate, and having experiences that fuel inspiration.

For several years, I had a practice of going in the water on the first of every month, but in December 2020 I started going in the water every day. There was

something about the sheer challenge of getting in the water when it was miserable outside—and also something incredibly special about swimming in the snow and also in the rain, feeling like you shouldn't be where you are, so exposed to the elements. There is nothing to do but just give in to your surroundings. The more I did it, the more I realized how good it made me feel. I kept going.

The water is different every day, and so is the tide, the weather, and the surroundings. So while getting into it is a daily ritual, the experience always feels distinct. I swim weekly with a group of women at a local boat launch, and a few of them have noted that even having spent decades living on our peninsula, the weekly cold-water practice has them thinking about their home in an entirely different way. I grew up here, and I feel exactly the same. Creative practice requires ritual, and while we often tend to think of inspiration as the result of new experiences (traveling, experiencing something new and unknown), I think that most often it's found when we can challenge our minds to look at something well known, and even mundane, in a new way.

When I head to the water, I know I am going to get a reset. No matter what is going on in my life or how cluttered my brain feels from juggling a variety of projects, getting into the water is like hitting the refresh button. I leave feeling more open and clear-headed.

I began these swims during a time in my life when I was facing some challenges, and while I didn't start going in the cold water to deal directly with those things, I can see now that it was an essential lifeline. The cold water continues to carry me through, both in high and low moments. As much as the water is a creative reset, it's also an emotional one.

In the cold, water freezes to ice. It's almost as if when you're in the cold water, all the stress and emotion coursing through your body does the same. And when it hardens, it's easier to break it into tiny, manageable pieces. It builds back up again of course, but for a short time, there's a release.

—ANNA BRONES

Merging

at the

Confluence

CHANNELING CHANGE

Christa is an urban farmer, social entrepreneur, and owner of FarmerJawn Greenhouses and CSA in Philadelphia. FarmerJawn follows regenerative farming practices that concentrate on soil health and increasing access to organic food for marginalized communities.

One of the many joys of my childhood was being a Girl Scout. I had the opportunity to learn how to canoe and I paddled on the Delaware River for hours at a time. I remember one of our trips being three

hours long; it was an amazing experience that boosted my confidence in my abilities outdoors, which was invaluable to me as a young Black woman. Being raised in the inner city, I recognize my privilege in

having these experiences to draw from, and I'm grateful for how they led me to where I am now.

I'm passionate about destigmatizing agriculture and creating safe spaces for us to engage in it. Agriculture doesn't get enough credit for how important it is and how it's the genesis of everything. All that we touch, what we drink, what we eat, the clothes that we wear, and the homes that we live in wouldn't exist without agriculture. And agriculture depends on water. No matter how folks mix it up—whether you use soil or focus only on hydroponics—water is essential to every single aspect of growing. Water is the driving force: a form of energy.

In a way, I channel this energy in my daily work as I strive to increase organic food-ways in urban environments and change the face of agriculture. Most of us are densely packed into cities, concrete jungles with blight everywhere. People have so many different thoughts about what farming is, or how they feel about soil, or the trauma that Black and Brown people have experienced in their connection to these things. Everyone deserves to feel comfortable and included in these spaces together—everyone should feel a sense of belonging. So, I get to function as a soluble agent to help dissolve colonized ways of thinking and naturalize people's practices. And in this I can assist in healing and creating peace, just as water does.

For me, regeneration is human-focused. If we are indeed the smartest beings on the planet, then it starts by us taking action. Everything is connected to everything, and we must understand that when we take care of the Earth, we take care of ourselves in the best way possible. I feel like my work allows me to be a beacon for people to believe that they have power to create change—regardless of what the world has told them. Everyone has the power to be more.

—CHRISTA BARFIELD

merging at the confluence

All ABOARD

Kayleen is a lifelong sailor, a commercial diver by trade, and a self-described subpar surfer. She lives aboard a 42-foot (12.8-metre) sailboat named *Footloose* on the coast of British Columbia, Canada, with plans to set sail for Mexico—or wherever the wind takes her.

Between diving, sailing, and living on a boat, I spend more time on and in water than on terra firma. I find a sense of peace in the chaos that the ocean brings (although the winter tends to test my limits). The more time I spend in and on the water, the more I find myself craving it. I started diving at thirteen but didn't turn it into a full-time career until after I'd spent six years in university and three years in an office marketing job. Commercial diving furthered my skill set in a marine environment, was financially rewarding, and provided more flexibility for me to go sailing when I want.

My job immerses me in another world, but not without the occasional danger, and I guess that's one of the reasons I changed careers—to find something that makes my heart race. I love the moment of jumping in when the world goes muffled and everything turns green. A bit of salt water drips down my mask and my drysuit starts to tighten up as I go deeper.

I've had moments of running out of air, my drysuit filling up with water, and even finding myself face-to-face with a wolf eel as long as me. These moments stick in my brain, but so does the time that a seal befriended me in a marina and nibbled on my fins, and the day I cruised down the strait with a pod of two hundred dolphins.

merging at the confluence

My job as a commercial diver takes me to many spots along the coast, but my favorite assignments are when I get to work on boats. Some of the most challenging yet rewarding jobs involve working with tools underwater. I've fixed sewer pipes in marinas, installed props on a bow thruster, and have changed many zincs on boats. People trust me to be their eyes and hands underwater, and I love being able to come out of the water and tell them the job is done.

Owning a boat myself has also been a truly rewarding experience. But for every sunny day with 15 knots on our beam, there's at least a couple of days with my head in the engine compart-ment, rewiring electrical and fixing leaking portlights.

The more work and time I spend on my boat, the more it loves me back and the more I trust her to take us to remote corners of the Pacific Ocean—like Hawai'i! Some years ago, my dad and I sailed to the Hawaiian Islands. Twenty-five days there. Twenty-four days back. Life became simple. The rolling ocean, the stars above us, the intense blue beneath us. There were so many special moments on that trip, but the feeling of simplicity and vulnerability is really what stuck with me.

—KAYLEEN VANDERREE

FINDING WORK ON THE WATER

by Olivia Klein

Olivia is the founder of Career Outdoors, which helps mission-driven
outdoor lovers by providing industry-specific resources, strategies,
and advice for creating a career in the outdoor and environmental sectors.

Whether you're a whitewater rafting enthusiast, enamored with ocean science, or curious about conservation work, it's possible to create a career path that allows you to spend time outdoors, impact the world, and turn your passion into a paycheck.

Water-based jobs may feel untraditional to some, but you'll discover that the options are quite robust. There are entire communities, dozens of sectors (including recreation, sciences, athletics, education, resources, fisheries, sustainability, and conservation), and opportunities across the globe. And, while you may be trading Wi-Fi for waders, you don't have to do it alone. Here are some tips to get you started in your very own fulfilling, water-based career.

CAREER CLARITY: There are a surprising number of jobs related to water sports and sciences. The first step is narrowing down which path you'd like to explore. You can find career clarity by journaling, researching job opportunities, volunteering, trying activities, and mentorship.

It's not important to narrow your career options to one specific path right away. Instead, the goal is to determine your interests, curiosities, financial and lifestyle goals, and the tasks that you do (and don't) enjoy. And remember—you're never tied to one path. You can always change your mind!

LOCATION: Although water jobs exist across the globe, you may have to relocate to begin, and accelerate, your career. For example, if you're excited about canoe guiding or fisheries science, it's important to live in an area where those industries exist!

Seasonal jobs are extremely common for entry-level candidates in water-related spaces, including roles in recreation, sciences, and water conservation. Although working seasonally can feel unstable, it's an incredible opportunity to travel and try new things.

GAINING EXPERIENCE: Now that you have an idea of which jobs are available to you, it's important to begin gaining experience. A great way to gain experience is by volunteering for local government agencies or nonprofits. You can participate in a river cleanup, join a community science study, or educate kids about the importance of our waterways. Volunteering allows you to discover your interests, gain qualifications to add to your resume, and network with like-minded people (and future employers)!

You may also consider internships, job shadowing, and accepting part-time work in the industry to gain valuable experience.

EDUCATION AND CERTIFICATIONS: You can also become a more competitive candidate through education and certifications. Evaluate the job opportunities that you are most excited about and begin reverse-engineering your career. Which certifications are required? How much education? What about skills? These questions will point you in the right direction and help you determine next steps.

JOB SEARCHING: There are two things that will help your job search go smoothly: consistency and industry-specific job boards.

The average job search takes three to six months, so consistency over time is important! Set aside time each week to search for new opportunities.

While general job boards, like Indeed, are great for some industries, outdoor employers rely on industry-specific sites to attract candidates. Here are some favorites:

- **SEVEN SEAS MEDIA OCEAN CONSERVATION JOBS LIST:** https://sevenseasmedia.org/ocean-jobs/

- **AMERICAN FISHERIES SOCIETY CAREER CENTER:** https://fisheries.org/employment/jobs/

- **JOSH'S WATER JOBS:** www.joshswaterjobs.com

- **ASSOCIATION OF ZOOS AND AQUARIUMS JOB BOARD:** https://www.aza.org/jobs

- **TEXAS A&M WILDLIFE AND FISHERIES SCIENCE JOB BOARD:** https://wfscjobs.tamu.edu/job-board/

- **CONSERVATION JOB BOARDS:** www.conservationjobboard.com

Creating a career that you're excited about can be a long journey. There will be snags and turns, drifts off course, and corrections—but it's always worth it to find rewarding work!

SEARCHING *for* the OCEAN *in the* MOUNTAINS

Sheri is the head designer and co-founder of Alpacka Raft. With over fifty years of experience as a product designer, Sheri leads with curiosity and a passion for all things outdoors.

I started waterskiing when I was in the seventh grade and I became a fanatic. I worked really hard at jumping, trick skiing, barefoot skiing, and slalom skiing. We also spent a few weeks every summer in the San Diego area, on the beach. Surfing was just being popularized in those days and I was hooked. I promised myself that when I got out of college I would move to the coast and become a great surfer—but life had different plans for me.

I chose to leave my home in Arizona and go to Oregon for college because I wanted to see if snow skiing was as much fun as waterskiing. It was, and then some: Snow skiing is why I moved to Jackson Hole after graduation. But if I wanted to live and ski in the mountains, I needed to find a way to support myself. I'd started making my own clothes in the fifth grade, so it felt second nature to create my own ski suit. And once I wore it on the slopes, the word spread. I called my company "Design by Sheri" and spent my days playing outdoors and my nights sewing.

But I really, really missed being around water. A few seasons into living in the mountains, I had the chance to go on a river trip in the Eastern Oregon desert country. It changed my life. There was one small Avon support raft (which I was on) and four kayakers. The kayakers let me play in their boats and I realized I could have most of what I loved about the ocean and surfing in the rivers of the mountains. I returned from this river trip and purchased what I believe to be the first whitewater kayak to show up in Jackson Hole. The rest, as they say, is history. I so clearly remember bouncing down the Hoback River by myself, happy as a clam, thinking, *This is the ocean in the mountains, and this is where I belong.*

In 1981, I moved with my then husband to Alaska and I sold "Design by Sheri." At the same time, I ended up developing chronic fatigue. When I got sick, kayaking was the sport I had to give up that hurt the most. I couldn't trust myself to be able to self-rescue, so I quit boating. I wasn't

merging at the confluence

willing to put the burden on someone else to save me if I got in trouble.

After seventeen years, I finally got treatment and started to feel like my old self again. In all that time, though, I always kept an eye on what was going on in the outdoor industry. So when my son Thor went on a 600-mile (965-kilometre) packrafting trip through the Brooks Range in Alaska, it really piqued my curiosity.

Packrafting is this wonderful meld of water and land. You're hiking, you're boating. A packraft is the epitome of a lightweight pack. If it weighs too much, you're not going to carry it. I'd never worked with inflatables before, but everything else about it connected with all I've ever done and cared about. After Thor returned from his trip, I couldn't believe the state his packraft was in. It was patches on top of patches. I was gawking at it when Thor said to me, "Mom, can you build me a boat?"

All of a sudden, this little light bulb started going off in me. It was that magic moment when my own body knew I was well enough to take on an entrepreneurial challenge again. I said yes, and Alpacka Raft was born in 2000.

Having my health come back and having my work involve water again in the form of packrafting was the greatest gift I could imagine. Yes, I love to hike, climb, run dogs, and ski, but being on the water has always been my greatest love.

—SHERI TINGEY

BROWN FOLKS FISHING

Tracy is an angler, crabber, and community conduit who's deeply passionate about advocating for social and environmental good. In 2018, Tracy founded Brown Folks Fishing—a community-based organization that is by and for Black, Indigenous, and People of Color (BIPOC) anglers—and works as a filmmaker, developing and producing independent documentary projects as well as commercial and branded content.

My parents are refugees from Vietnam. The ocean, rivers, fish, and water buffalo were all part of stories they would tell me—snippets of memories I never lived as their American-born daughter. Fishing, camping, and crabbing were a big part of my childhood. My family didn't have a lot, so these activities made for an easy and affordable way to get together outdoors.

After college, I casually fished here and there, but it wasn't until later that I really rekindled my connection to the water. I became obsessed with salmon and steelhead fishing but didn't have anyone to show me the ropes, so I started searching around online. That's when I began to acknowledge the broader, popular culture around fishing. Having done my graduate work in conflict studies with a focus on restorative justice, I got back into fishing with an intersectional lens of how that applied to the sport—especially for me as

a queer woman of color who presents as gender nonconforming.

The public face of recreational fishing is predominantly white and male, but I knew from growing up in Portland and living in LA that it wasn't reflective of reality. On any given weekend you'll find Black and Brown families at lakes, rivers, piers, and ponds. Many of our communities have deeply rooted lifeways and traditions in fishing. I knew there had to be more folks out there who felt similarly, were looking for other BIPOC folks to fish with, or didn't have access and needed a safer space to start. So I launched Brown Folks Fishing to send up a flare and see who else was out there. I wanted to create a space that very intentionally surfaced and centered the faces and stories of anglers of color.

Brown Folks Fishing has allowed people to finally see themselves reflected with no

merging at the confluence

requirement of how to be on the water. It's provided a way for folks from across the country to connect, communicate, collaborate, and link up to go fishing. Early on in our development, a good friend posed the question, "What does it look like to bring our full selves to the water?" and that's guided our work ever since. Every narrative shared within our community is part of the ever-expanding answer to that question.

Being on the water with other anglers of color stokes joy for me. We don't even need to see a fish. It's just about sharing those moments with each other—just as we are, free from any gaze, and unencumbered by others' expectations. When we're able to bring our full selves to those places, that's when we begin to truly feel free.

—TRACY NGUYEN-CHUNG

The WAY WATER CONNECTS *Us*

Dani is a Mestiza-API athlete and storyteller driven to rewrite the narrative of who belongs outside. As someone who spends much of her time climbing, skiing, splitboarding, and running in the mountains, she is constantly in search of new routes and fresh tracks, as well as opportunities to share about Mother Earth's most impacted places.

Water feels like coming home. Growing up, water was a place to play, pray, cry, and heal. It's the most important element in my life, the one that leads me to joy. And yet, it's also the one that has become scarcer, year after year.

As a splitboarder, I want to have a safe and solid snow path. I want to have a community of people that I can ski and splitboard with that are positive and supportive. I want to be able to have good food on my table. And all these things are linked.

Our relationship with other animals and humans, with the land, and with our food has made it clear to me—more so than ever before—that we are deeply tied to the cycles through which water moves. Water is what connects us. The sooner we build a relationship with water, the sooner we can start to recognize all it gives us, so that we may begin to give back.

Part of my work is advocating for doing what's right. And if we go back to the idea of collective liberation—the recognition that all our struggles are intimately connected—it's important to identify the ways we can show up for all communities. Because unless we're thinking about everyone, then we're really just thinking about ourselves, and that kind of mindset doesn't serve anyone.

As a woman, and particularly as a woman of color, I'm honored to have the opportunity to work alongside the living legends at Protect Our Winters. I'm excited to use my voice to advocate for the environment and urge people to adopt an interrelationship with the Earth—one that embraces the concept of collective action in hopes of a better future for all of us.

—DANI REYES-ACOSTA

The POWER of STORYTELLING

Brianne is the descendant of Filipino plantation workers who immigrated to Hawai'i in the early 1900s, and is the daughter, granddaughter, and great-granddaughter of local fishers and hunters. She began spearfishing and diving at a young age, but it was later in life, home from college during the pandemic, that she began fishing and spear-fishing in earnest. Brianne is a first-generation college student and Truman and Udall Scholar. A storyteller for her family, Brianne documents and preserves the knowledge and life stories of her loved ones, past and present.

It's said that a person's hands reveal a lot about them—and the hands of my great-grandfather told that he was a fisherman.

As a young boy, my uncle had observed his hands. Decades later, he still recalls with the fascination of a child how my great-grandfather had no fingerprints. With his bare hands, my great-grandfather dropped down and pulled up his fishing line so many times, that where it rested was made smooth and thin, rubbed free of any lines.

I come from a fishing family. When my paternal relatives came to Hawai'i from the Philippines, they were drawn to the waters of the ocean and depended on it for many of their needs. Their children, and their children's children, became fishers as well. I'd like to say I carried on their traditions from early in life. But that didn't happen for me. I began fishing much later—but neither from the pull of the ocean's waters or for survival. Rather, I did it because of stories.

Months before I started fishing, I sat with the elders of my family and listened to their stories. My visits with them were sparked by a reality that shook me: I knew nothing of those who had come before me. I barely knew their names.

One of the people I listened to was my uncle Lance Lauro (my father's brother). He was a gifted storyteller and fisherman. Through his stories, I could see people I'd

merging at the confluence

never laid eyes on. I could envision them: their nature, their tone of voice, their character . . . all by what he said.

When he spoke of both my great-grandfather and grandfather, he told of how they were great fishermen. He had seen them fish and learned from them too. He was the one who told me the story of my great-grandfather's hands.

But then one day I asked myself: What would happen after my uncle? No one else on my father's side knew how to fish. I was the oldest of my siblings, and my uncle had no kids. He was the very last one. After him, there would be no fishers.

I decided to take up fishing to see for myself the things that my uncle described in his stories—and to carry on my family's knowledge and tradition too.

The more I've done it, the more I understand each of their lives—the lives of fishermen, and the lives of those deeply connected to the ocean.

And so, when I fish all night with my uncle beneath the stars, the white, braided line moving between my fingertips, damp with saltwater, I think of my great-grandfather, my grandfather, and all those who have loved the ocean before me.

—BRIANNE DEWANI LAURO

INTRODUCING LITTLE ONES TO WATER

Water is a dynamic playground for all ages, but it can hold special wonder for young ones just getting acquainted with it. From sidewalk puddles to public pools, rock-studded creeks and the shallows of alpine lakes, water offers new dimensions, challenges, and opportunities for movement and learning. But it can also hold dangers, so dealing with safety concerns must be factored into this introduction.

START WITH PLAY: Building a relationship with water might begin in the bathtub or on a rainy-day walk, and the exposure is cumulative. Shallower realms are a perfect place to gauge comfort level and interest. Does your child hate getting their face wet? Does cold bother them? Are they curious about the way water moves? Baths and water tables are also a great place to explore the sensory aspects of water and to gain confidence in playing with water toys, cups, and splashing.

LEARN TO SWIM: The American Academy of Pediatrics doesn't recommend that children begin formal swimming lessons until age four, but starting around age one, it's possible for children to learn rescue techniques like floating in a setting such as infant self-rescue swim classes, which is an incredible basis for water safety. When seeking lessons for kids of any age, look for certified instructors who teach classes focused on both swimming skills and water survival.

SUPPORT THE INDIVIDUAL: Whenever you're taking children into water environments, especially if you're not their primary caregiver, it's important to know their experience and comfort level. Have they had swimming lessons? Are they afraid of falling in? Does breath-holding cause anxiety? Any of these things (and others) can increase safety concerns, on top of inhibiting the enjoyment of an activity. Early positive experiences in water of all kinds can serve as a foundation for a lifelong relationship brimming with possibilities.

CONSIDER GEAR AND ENVIRONMENTAL SAFETY: As vital as it is to have a good basis in swimming techniques and self-rescue, it's also necessary to gear up and dress appropriately for all water activities. This might mean always using personal floatation devices where recommended, making sure snorkels or goggles are in good condition,

following posted instructions at pools and parks, and staying aware of conditions if they might change—like surging waves at a beach.

Environmental safety can also include responding to how crowded a pool is, if there are currents or tides, whether there's a lifeguard on duty, and how cold the water is. It's important to both understand this as a guardian and communicate it to the children, so everyone is on the same page about hazards and how to respond.

EMBRACE VARIETY: For older children who might not be confident or interested in swimming, there are still so many engaging water activities to try. Playing in sprinklers, wading, paddling, or learning about fish and aquatic wildlife can all be super-enriching sensory experiences in a variety of different waterscapes or urban settings.

SUSTAINING TRADITIONAL KNOWLEDGE

Marina is a leader in the Haida and Lingít community on what is known as Prince of Wales Island in southeast Alaska, where the Tongass National Forest kisses the sea. She heads her tribal government and serves on many boards and committees, working to protect traditional waters and lands.

The way we love our unborn children is the love the water has always shown me. My relationship with water is multigenerational and long-term. I grew up right against the ocean and still go to the water daily for strength and healing. I have always held deep respect for the element that not only provides sustenance but also lessons that we must carefully learn.

Our foods, medicines, and materials come from the land and water. With Western contact, our sovereignty was ignored, and therefore our land and water left our stewardship. We are working to reclaim the rights to steward our traditional lands and waters to restore their health and bring balance back to their ecosystems. When we reclaim stewardship, we can also reclaim our traditional foods and medicines by ensuring the sustainability of the harvesting.

My entire upbringing revolved around food and family. If we weren't having a big feast, we were out harvesting or sharing our harvest.

Today my most cherished moments are when I am in the smokehouse where my late father used to hang our fish and deer. However, when I was growing up, my entire family would stay at our house while we caught and processed fish, processed berries, and more. I remember taking grocery sacks out with my cousin to fill them with elderberries and fishing with my father and the crew.

I can close my eyes and picture sitting at the table with my mom, grandmother, and cousins squeezing salmon into jars. My grandmother's gold nugget bracelet would *clink-clank* on the table as she cut the salmon into smaller pieces. My cousins and I tried to keep up with her but would get mesmerized in the *Tetris* puzzle of packing the fish tightly into the jars. "Wipe the rims good!" our grandmother would remind us far too often.

As a Haida and Lingít woman born into this generation, I am humbly proud of every bit of traditional knowledge that I carry—of harvesting and food preservation, carving, weaving, beading, fur and skin sewing, and storytelling. By all odds I should not exist, and the traditional knowledge I hold should not exist. The illegalization of our traditional ways of life meant that my ancestors were actively being criminals in their attempt to retain our ancient knowledge and ways of living. These "skills" keep us in balance with the rest of our ecosystem and will continue to do so for generations to come.

As people of the sea I find it important for us to remember the ingenuity and strength of our ancestors and their voyages in our dugout canoes. A traditional dugout canoe requires a particular type of tree, a detailed method, and plenty of strength to carve, steam, and bend it. Our canoes took us farther than Western scholars could imagine, and the canoes were powered by the strength of our people.

When we are at sea, there are times where the cresting silvery-black waves smash against each other, and it is then that we must paddle harder to keep moving forward. The recent history of our people is a painful one, but by referring to the canoe often, I am able to pull the memory strength and steer the canoe that holds the stories of us Lingít and Haida peoples in the right direction.

—MARINA ANDERSON

THANKS

A book about women and water could not be possible without our many teachers. Thank you forever to my dad, for slathering on my sunscreen, lacing my hockey skates, and untangling my fishing line. Thank you to my mom for seeing infinite colors in sunsets at the lake. I'm grateful to my sister and brother for the water memories, new and old, and to my niece and nephew, Sloane and Hampton, who are never not ready for a swim. Thanks to Gabaccia Moreno for piquing my curiosity about fly-fishing. Big thanks to our Chronicle Books editors, Rachel Hiles and Claire Gilhuly, for shaping these words with the delicate touch of a river. And to my partner, Jon Gaffney, for modeling his passion for all things watersports (even if it meant us lugging a waterski around the country).

—GS

Thank you to my grandparents, who carted fishing poles, bug nets, and inner tubes on all our summer adventures and showed me how to bait a hook and follow the gentle tug of curiosity. I hold depths of gratitude to my husband, Jesse, who's always up for a swim no matter how cold the water is; my mom for the endless supply of watercolor paints; and my sister Rachel for always paddling on the other half of the raft and keeping me afloat in so many ways. The energy I got to pour into this book would also not have been possible without Shauna Neill and all the other caregivers who held my child while I dove into these stories.

—HH

Thank you to my mom, who encouraged my early obsession with aquatic adventures and obliged my steadfast commitment to always be the last one out of the water after sundown. Thank you to my abuelo Quintero for placing a fishing pole in my tiny hands the moment I learned to walk. Thank you to Coach Lyons for ensuring that I always caught a glimpse of a supportive face every time I turned to breathe during a race. Thank you to Mr. Rose, who spent as much time coaching me to swim better as he did coaching me to write better. And thank you to Terry Beck, for teaching me how to introduce others, gently and graciously, to the joy of swimming and in turn taught me how to be gentle and gracious with myself too.

—NR

CONTRIBUTORS

Contributors' websites and Instagram handles provided, unless otherwise specified.

MARINA ANDERSON
@marina_alaska
marinaalaska.com

CHRISTA "FARMERJAWN" BARFIELD
@farmerjawnphilly
farmerjawnphilly.com

RACHEL BARRETT
@luminousandwild,
@northprestonsurf &
@texturedwaves

MORGAN BATTEY
@morganbattey

BIRDEE (JAMIE JOHNSON)
@bird.ee
www.bird.ee

IMANI BLACK
@imaniiiblackkk &
@mia_npo

ANNA BRONES
@annabrones
annabrones.com
creativefuelcollective.com

KARIN BROWNE
@karinbrowne

MICHELLE COLSON
Instagram, TikTok:
@guardianofthesprings

GINA ROSA COVA
@ginarosacova
ginacova.com

INKA CRESSWELL
@inkacresswell
inkacresswell.com

EDEN ELGETI
@thetransgenderswimmer

SOPHIA EUGENE
@sprinkleofsophia

MUGDHA FLORES
@mugsie_b

CLAIRE GIORDANO
@claireswanderings
adventureartacademy.com

MICHAELA GOADE
@michaelagoade
michaelagoade.com

HEATHER HANSMAN
@hhansman
heatherhansman.com

SOFIA JIN
@sofjin_
sofiajin.com

JAMIE KISH
@girlinwaterphotography
girlinwater.com

OLIVIA KLEIN
@careeroutdoors career-outdoors.com

LAURA KOTTLOWSKI
Instagram: @laurakottlowski
TikTok: @laura.kottlowski
laurakottlowski.com

BRIANNE DEWANI LAURO
Instagram: @brianne_lauro
Facebook: Brianne Lauro

ANTOINETTE LEE TOSCANO
@antoinetteleetoscano
antoinettetoscano.com
xotv.me channels/359-whitewatertv

PENNY MABIE
Instagram: @pennymabie
Facebook: PennyMabie

ASH MANNING
Instagram:
@AshleysAdventure
TikTok: Ashleysadventure_
ashleysadventure.com

IRENE MARCOUX
@irene_la_sirene

ZANDILE NDHLOVU
Instagram, TikTok, Facebook, Twitter: @zandithemermaid &
@theblackmermaid_foundation

TRACY NGUYEN-CHUNG
@brownfolksfishing
brownfolksfishing.com

LIZZY RAGAN
@lizzy.ragan &
@lizzyraganart
lizzyraganart.com

KASIE REGNIER
@kasieregs &
@maddy_the_mess

DANI REYES-ACOSTA
@notlostjustdiscovering
danireyesacosta.com

JUDITH SADORA
@triunehealthandwellness
 triunehealthandwellness.com

NIKKI SMITH
@nikkik_smith
nikkismith.com

CARIN TERESA
@swimawaythepain

SHERI TINGEY
@alpacka_raft
alpackaraft.com

BONNIE TSUI
Instagram: @BonnieTsui8
Twitter: @BonnieTsui
bonnietsui.com

LARISSA VAN DER LAAN
@anda.designstore

OLIVIA VANDAMME
@olivialomasi & @livs.wav

KAYLEEN VANDERREE
@fromsnowtosail &
@allaboutspray

YOLANDE WEBSTER
@sistah_soulja89

KATIE WILEY
@thekitchenwild

CREDITS

2–3: Photograph by Jesse Newmarch; Featuring Hailey Hirst

5, 6: Photographs by and featuring Noël Russell

8, 9: Photographs by Gale Straub

11: Photograph by Gale Straub; Featuring Gale Straub

12: Photograph by Rachel Iverson; Featuring Hailey Hirst

15: Photograph by and featuring Noël Russell

16–17: Photograph by Noël Russell

18: Photograph by Gale Straub

21: Photograph by Hailey Hirst

22–23: Photograph by Gale Straub

24: Photograph by and featuring Noël Russell

27–29: Photographs provided by and featuring Karin Browne

30: Photograph by Katy Weaver; Featuring Lizzy Ragan

32: Artwork by Lizzy Ragan

33: Photograph by Katy Weaver; Featuring Lizzy Ragan; Artwork by Lizzy Ragan

34: Photograph by Katy Weaver; Featuring Lizzy Ragan

35: Artwork by Lizzy Ragan

37: Photograph by Seattle Dive Tours; Featuring Mugdha Flores

38: Photograph by Ocean Exploration Trust; Featuring Mugdha Flores

39: Photograph by James Flores; Featuring Mugdha Flores

41: Photograph by Gale Straub; Featuring Julie Hotz

42: Photograph by Gale Straub; Featuring Heidi Annalise

44, 46, 47: Photographs courtesy of and featuring Gina Rosa Cova

49, 50: Photographs by Mike Battey; Featuring Morgan Battey

51: Photograph by Kelly Grow featuring Morgan Battey

53: Photographs by and featuring Noël Russell

54: Photograph by Glen Iverson; Featuring Rachel Iverson

55: Photographs by Hailey Hirst (L) and Noël Russell (R)

56: Photograph by Dela Inomwan; Featuring Sophia Eugene

58: Photograph by and featuring Sophia Eugene

59: Photograph by Angelica Romero; Featuring Sophia Eugene

60: Photograph by Gale Straub

63: Photograph by Birdee; Featuring Stella De Mont

64–65, 66, 67: Photographs by Birdee; Featuring Emily Moss

71: Photograph by Piece of Time Photography; Featuring Michelle Colson

72–73: Photograph by Josh Hansbrough; Featuring Michelle Colson

74, 75: Photographs by Piece of Time Photography; Featuring Michelle Colson

77, 78: Photographs courtesy of and featuring Kasie Regnier

79: Photograph by Hailey Hirst

80, 81: Photographs by Gale Straub

83: Photograph by Frances Duncan; Featuring Bonnie Tsui

84: Photograph by Melissa Gibson; Featuring Bonnie Tsui

85: Photograph by Marine Jaud, Callum Morse of Surf Simply; Featuring Bonnie Tsui

87, 88–89: Photographs courtesy of and featuring Irene Marcoux

91, 92–93: Photographs by Luke Cresswell; Featuring Inka Cresswell

94, 95: Photographs by Inka Cresswell

96, 98: Photographs by Jacki Bruniquel; Featuring Zandile Ndhlovu

99: Photograph by Nicolene Olckers; Featuring Zandile Ndhlovu

100–101: Photograph by Jacki Bruniquel; Featuring Zandile Ndhlovu

102: Photograph by Noël Russell

105, 106–107: Photographs by and featuring Carin Teresa

109: Photograph by Noël Russell

111: Photograph by Kate Crump; Featuring Penny Mabie

112: Photograph by Heather Hodson; Featuring Penny Mabie

114: Photograph provided by and featuring Katie Wiley

116–117: Photograph by Jeremy Burke @j.burkephotos and featuring Katie Wiley

119, 120, 121: Photographs by Charlie Bush of 2B13 Productions; Featuring Eden Elgeti

122, 124: Photographs by Bethany Goodrich; Featuring

Michaela Goade and artwork by Michaela Goade

125: Photograph courtesy of and featuring Michaela Goade

127, 128-129: Photographs by Aslan Steel; Featuring Sofia Jin

130, 132, 133: Photographs by and featuring Judith Sadora

135, 137: Photographs by Matthew James Berrafato; Featuring Antoinette Lee Toscano

138-139: Photograph by Gale Straub

140, 142, 143: Photographs by Caroline J. Phillips; Featuring Imani Black

144: Photograph by Noël Russell

146: Photograph by and featuring Laura Kottlowski

148-149: Photograph by Sarah Seibold; Featuring Laura Kottlowski

150: Photograph by and featuring Laura Kottlowski

151: Photograph by Marisa Jarae; Featuring Laura Kottlowski

152: Photograph by Chip Sanders; Featuring Ash Manning

154-155: Photograph courtesy of and featuring Ash Manning

157: Photograph courtesy of and featuring Heather Hansman

158, 159: Photographs by Hailey Hirst

160: Photograph by Brandy Clark @brandyland80; Featuring Yolande Webster

164, 165: Photographs by Noye Kim (they/them); Featuring Olivia VanDamme

167: Photograph by and featuring Larissa van der Laan

168, 169: Artwork by Larissa van der Laan

170: Photograph by Jill Cluett; Featuring Rachel Barrett

172, 173: Photographs by Karl Funk; Featuring Rachel Barrett

175: Photograph by Jake Hirschi; Featuring Nikki Smith

176-177, 178: Self Portraits by Nikki Smith - Pullphotography

179: Photograph by Jake Hirschi; Featuring Nikki Smith

180: Photograph by and featuring Jamie Kish

182: Photograph by Jamie Kish

183: Photograph by Lauren Strach; Featuring Jamie Kish

184-185: Photograph by Jamie Kish

186: Photograph by Virginia Giordano; Featuring Claire Giordano

187: Artwork by Claire Giordano

188: Photograph by Virginia Giordano; Featuring Claire Giordano

189: Photograph by and featuring Claire Giordano

190: Photograph by and featuring Anna Brones

191: Art and photograph by Anna Brones

192: Photograph by Eric Olsen; Featuring Anna Brones

193: Photograph by Luc Revel; Featuring Anna Brones

194: Photograph by Noël Russell

196, 197: Photographs by and featuring Christa "FarmerJawn" Barfield

198: Photograph by Tyler Turner; Featuring Kayleen VanderRee

199, 200: Photographs by Abby Cooper; Featuring Kayleen VanderRee

201: Photograph by Kayleen VanderRee

203: Photographs by and featuring Olivia Klein

205: Photograph by James Flores; Featuring Mugdha Flores

206: Photograph courtesy of and featuring Sheri Tingey

209: Photograph by Noël Russell

210: Photograph by Matty Wong; Featuring Tracy Nguyen-Chung

212-213: Photograph by Tracy Nguyen-Chung

214: Photograph by Nick Raingsey; Featuring Tracy Nguyen-Chung

215: Photographs by Tracy Nguyen-Chung

216-217: Photograph by Hailey Hirst

218: Photograph by and featuring Dani Reyes-Acosta

220: Photograph courtesy of Brianne Dewani Lauro

222, 223: Photographs courtesy of Lance Lauro and featuring Brianne Dewani Lauro

225, 226, 227: Photographs by Hailey Hirst; Featuring Rachel Iverson and Cassidy Newmarch

228, 230: Photographs by and featuring Marina Anderson

232-233: Photograph by Hailey Hirst

234: Photograph by and featuring Noël Russell

237: Photograph by Gale Straub

244: Photograph by Hailey Hirst

credits